FAILURE to FILE

How to get the nonfiler back on track

- COLLECTION
- COMPROMISE
- IRS NOTICE
- LIEN/LEVY

James E. Jenkins, CPA

Tax Research Services, Inc.
Southfield, Michigan

Additional copies of this book may be ordered by sending $12.95 plus $3.50 for postage and handling to:
Publishers Distribution Service
6893 Sullivan Road
Grawn, MI 49637
(800) 345-0096

Copyright © 1994 by James E. Jenkins

All rights reserved. No part of this book may be reproduced, by any means, without permission in writing from the publisher, except by a reviewer who wishes to quote brief excerpts in connection with a review in a magazine or newspaper. For information contact: Tax Research Services, Inc., 17288 W. Twelve Mile, Southfield, MI 48076.

Publisher's Cataloging-in-Publication Data

Jenkins, James E.,
    Failure to file : how to get the nonfiler back on
  track : collection, compromise, IRS notice, lien/levy /
  by James E. Jenkins—Southfield, Michigan : Tax
  Research Services, Inc.
      p.   ill.   cm.
  Includes index.
  ISBN: 0-9639488-0-6
  1. Income tax—United States—Popular works. 2. Tax Evasion—United States—Popular works. 3. Tax collection—United States—Popular works. I. Title.
HJ4653.E75J   1994
343.73'052'04—dc20   93-61768

Manufactured in the United States of America.

10 9 8 7 6 5 4 3 2 1

Text Developed by Jill E. Rybka/PDS

Book Design by Laura Argyle/PDS

*To my wife, Peggy, for all her support,
and to my sons,
Eric, Jeff, Greg and Steve.*

Contents

Exhibits	ix
Preface	xi
Introduction	xv
Acknowledgments	xvii

PART ONE

1 THE FIRST STEP — 3-16
Who Are Nonfilers? • The Nonfiling Syndrome
Three Main Reasons for Not Filing • Case Studies
Saddam Hussein Syndrome

2 GETTING WITH THE PROGRAM — 19-37
How the Nonfiler Program Works • Locating
the Nonfiler • Initial Contact • 10 Day Letter
30 Day Letter • 90 Day Letter • Collectable Liability
The Summons Power • Criminal Intent

3 THE IMPORTANCE OF AN OVERALL STRATEGY — 59-68
Employing a Tax Professional • Going it Alone
Assessing the Damage • Understanding Statutes
Buying Time • Gathering Information
Tax Organizer • Missing Information

4 RESPONDING TO IRS TACTICS — 71-87
Tax Court Petition • Penalties • Waiver of Penalties
Case Studies • Levy • Lien

5 PREFILING STRATEGIES — 89-102
Various Filing Categories • Case Studies
Levying Bank Accounts • The Friendly Lien
Obtaining Tax Forms

PART TWO

6 DEALING WITH COLLECTIONS — 105-127
Collection Information Statement • Collection
Automated Collections • Buying Time
Failed Payment Arrangements • Case Study

7 OFFER IN COMPROMISE — 129-147
The Offer Period • Advantage to the Offer
Disadvantage to the Offer • Timing of the Offer
The Offer Amount • Other Considerations
Appeals and Resubmission

8 BANKRUPTCY — 149-157
Chapter Seven • The Automatic Stay
Chapter Thirteen • Case Studies
Chapter "Twenty" • The Bankruptcy Attorney

9 HELP WHEN YOU NEED IT — 159-161
Tax Research Services, Inc.

Glossary — 163-167
Index — 169-170

Exhibits

Reminder of Unpaid Tax	23
Have You Filed Your Tax Return?	24
Overdue Tax	25
Urgent—Payment Required	26
Notice of Intent to Levy	27
10-Day Letter	29
30-Day Letter	30
90 Day Letter	31
Summons, Form 2039	34
Request for Copy of Tax Form, Form 4506	48
Tax Organizer	52
Petition	74
Designation of Place of Trial	75
Release of Levy, Form 668-D	83
Notice of Federal Tax Lien, Form 668-F	87
Collection Information Statement for Individuals, Form 433-A	109
Collection Information Statement for Businesses, Form 433-B	113
Installment Agreement Request, Form 9465	118
Defaulted Installment Agreement	126
Offer in Compromise, Form 656	132
Appeal of Offer Letter	141
Power of Attorney & Declaration of Representative, Form 2848	145
IRS Letter	147

Preface

IN EARLY 1992 I met a couple that related a tragic story. Don was a self-employed carpenter who had fallen on hard times during the recession of the early eighties. His wife, Carol (pregnant with their third child) worked at a number of odd jobs just to make ends meet. With their debt mounting, credit cards at their limit, and two months behind in house payments, Don and Carol decided not to file their income tax returns, thinking they could resume filing the following year. However, the next year was no better. In fact, the situation continued for three years before Don and Carol decided to seek professional help.

In 1984 they contacted a bankruptcy attorney who advised them they could start life anew by filing for personal bankruptcy. The attorney also referred the couple to a CPA for the preparation of their tax returns, which he filed with a tax liability of $22,000. In the meantime, the attorney filed for bankruptcy on Don and Carol's behalf, discharging all outstanding debts - *except their taxes*. Because this case was not handled properly, the bankruptcy did not include or eliminate the state and federal income taxes, and the ensuing interest and penalties have continued to mount.

Don and Carol are financially ruined. They lost their home and even ten years later find they are unable to obtain credit cards or purchase a home or automobile. Also, the IRS is now threatening to levy their wages unless the couple agree to extend the normal statute of limitations period by an extra five years, perpetuating their already dismal existence.

This didn't have to happen. Because these two professionals - the CPA and the bankruptcy attorney - did not combine their knowledge of the tax laws and bankruptcy statutes, Don and Carol have paid an incredible price. In fact, Don and Carol could have fared much better had they themselves possessed some understanding of tax law and strategy, and had known how to choose a competent CPA and lawyer.

If this story sounds familiar, this book is for you. Or, perhaps you've purchased this book for a friend or loved one in a similar nonfiling situation. Whatever the case, help is available.

I've been a Certified Public Accountant for twenty-two years and during that time handled over 1,000 nonfiling cases. I've seen absolute horror stories. But I've also seen seemingly hopeless tax situations turned around, incurring minimal financial damage, simply by applying my knowledge of tax law, bankruptcy law and initiating a working strategy. That's why I wrote this book.

I believe that every nonfiler situation has a solution, no matter how bleak. By gaining knowledge of statutes, IRS policy, asset-protecting strategies and more, you'll be able to get through your tax plight, resume a timely tax paying system, and stay there.

The Internal Revenue Service is not a government agency to tackle alone and without guidance. If you are involved in a nonfiling situation, it is extremely important to take the initiative and address the issue. The contents of this book could very well spell the difference between your financial life and death.

Introduction

Have you been afraid to answer a knock at your door? Do you screen all phone calls and refuse certified mail? Are you a literal prisoner in your own home, peering cautiously outside at a strange car in your driveway? Do you sometimes feel you are being watched or followed? If these "nonfiling symptoms" sound familiar, you're not alone. The IRS calculates an approximate 10 million people in this country who are delinquent in their taxes, resulting in a loss to the budget of $7 to $10 billion dollars. That's serious money, and that's why the IRS introduced a program in October of 1992 designed to "reel-in" nonfilers.

If you are delinquent in your taxes and haven't as yet been contacted by the IRS, chances are you will be. The delay usually isn't that the IRS hasn't detected the nonfiler, they're simply a huge branch of the Government and are incredibly slow.

This book assumes that you, the reader, are a nonfiler; an individual who has fallen behind in his or her filing of income tax returns and payment of such taxes. It also assumes that your situation has become intolerable and you wish to do something about it. This book is designed to help you successfully maneuver through the many obstacles inherent in a nonfiling situation, with as little financial loss as possible, and help you resume a timely tax filing system.

This book is not meant to help an individual elude the IRS, but rather to address a nonfiling situation, restore some sanity to your life, and protect now and future assets. It should also be used as a supplement when employing a tax professional.

This book is written for the layman. It is not a textbook. It is conversational in tone and relies much on personal experience, examples and strategies, using case studies and illustrations.

This book is presented in two parts; the *prefiling section* and *postfiling section.* In the prefiling section, we will discuss topics such as how the nonfiler program works, responses to IRS tactics such as levy, lien and the summons power, and developing an overall strategy, as well as isolated asset-protecting strategies.

In the second, or postfiling, section we will discuss dealing with collections, failed payment arrangements, the offer in compromise and appeals and bankruptcy options, as well as more strategies and case studies. The last chapter details ways to choose competent CPA's and lawyers to give you the most professional help available. There is also a glossary of terms and an index to help you quickly locate information in answer to pressing questions.

For clarification, you will find that this book is written primarily in the masculine form and the majority of case study characters will also be male. This is simply because nonfiling males outnumber nonfiling females approximately four to one.

Acknowledgments

M‌y thanks to the staff at Tax Research Services, Inc. for their important contributions. My special thanks to Don Schippa, Diane Randolph, EA and David Wagner, CPA.

FAILURE to FILE

ONE

Prefiling Section

Well, fancy giving money to the Government!
Might as well have put it down the drain.
Fancy giving money to the Government!
Nobody will see the stuff again.
Well, they've no idea what money's for -
Ten to one they'll start another war.
I've heard a lot of silly things, but Lor'!
Fancy giving money to the Government.
    - A.P. Herbert

1

The First Step

SIT DOWN. TAKE a deep breath. Relax.

I'm serious. You've probably been suffering a great deal of stress due to your nonfiling situation - possibly even been on the verge of an emotional break-down. It's not unusual. You probably think about your predicament every single day. The overt and covert stress can be emotionally and physically exhausting.

You probably feel isolated, alone, and afraid. Not only aren't you able to openly talk with others about your nonfiling fears because of shame, feelings of guilt and the fear the IRS may find out, but you are probably also in a "bad space" financially and emotionally. Failing to file tax returns is usually the result of some personal misfortune, whether it be a death in the family, divorce, failed business, loss of a job, or bankruptcy. Not to mention that you won't be getting too much sympathy from your friends or family even if you *did* tell them about your predicament, because they may feel slighted that you aren't paying your taxes and they are. Certainly, the IRS will not be sympathetic with you. However, it is not my job (nor any tax professionals job) to judge you. Personal misfortunes simply happen. The only thing to do is deal with the problem as best you can.

Dealing with the IRS is an intimidating matter. They are a large and powerful branch of our Government and, in most cases, the laws favor them. But right now, you're allowed to breathe a sigh of relief. True, your problems haven't as yet been solved, but by reading this book you've taken that first, important step to remedying your tax, and therefore financial, situation.

Who Are Nonfilers?

For the most part, nonfilers have no criminal intent, though a small portion are actual tax protestors. Interestingly, one in seven nonfilers are income tax preparers, accountants, CPA's, and lawyers - so don't feel too out-of-place. Ninety-eight percent of nonfilers are average Americans who stopped filing their returns because of some sort of financial or emotional crisis. In most cases, both factors are present. However, even though you probably have no criminal intent nor are you looking to deliberately defraud the U.S. Government, you *can* be prosecuted criminally by the Government for failing to file your taxes.

Usually the problem that originally kept you from filing dissipates rather quickly, but then you find yourself in a catch-22 situation. There is the initial assumption that when this particular problem has passed you can "catch-up". However, when April 15th rolls around again, you're hesitant to file the current years taxes for fear of alerting the IRS that you didn't file the previous year's returns, either. (Though the IRS is probably already aware of it - they just haven't contacted you as yet.) Pretty soon this situation snowballs. Before long - especially with interest and penalties - your tax liability has grown to a completely unmanageable size.

The Nonfiling Syndrome

Often times, people feel that they are completely alone and isolated in their problems - especially regarding a nonfiling situation, because you aren't apt to share this fact with too many people. You begin to feel like an exile in your own country.

Dealing with the IRS can be a frightening experience. This fear is probably intensified by your own feelings of guilt because, after all, you are just a decent citizen who has fallen behind in their taxes - probably not a tax-dodging criminal. Most of my nonfiling clients have suffered a great deal of mental anguish before they finally sought professional tax help. They develop minor to extreme feelings of paranoia, depression and anxiety; afraid to answer a knock at the door, peering through drawn curtains at strange cars parked outside their homes, and the feeling that they are being followed. Nonfilers enter into their own private hell.

Case Study:

Ted and Diane lived in Hawaii - a place you'd consider a wonderful paradise. However, Ted and Diane lived in constant turmoil because Ted hadn't filed his income taxes in 6 years. Ted knew he owed the government money, but he also knew he couldn't pay such a large tax liability so the situation just continued year after year. It got to the point where this predicament completely overshadowed his life. He was a complete wreck. He hid indoors with the curtains pulled, wouldn't answer the door, refused all certified mail, and was afraid to go out to eat for fear an IRS or FBI agent was sitting nearby. Diane finally left him.

Case Study:

Tina was responsible for filing her family's income tax returns and had told her husband, Joe, that their financial matters were up to date. However, the truth was she'd been filing extensions for 5 years. Tina had been suffering from extreme depression; she gained an extra 40 or 50 pounds, screened all phone calls, refused all certified mail, and had been literally hiding out in her home.

Tina did send the IRS some money over the years, but it was well below what she knew they really owed. The IRS began sending letters to Tina and Joe, but Tina tried desperately to hide the situation from her husband. Finally, the IRS started sending some really threatening letters and Tina had to confess the truth to Joe. The two of them finally came into my office.

Having considered all available options and deciding on a course of action, we were able to manage the IRS tax debt with minimal damage. In fact, simply coming forward with this terrible secret seemed to do Tina a world of good. She eventually lost the 40 or 50 pounds and looked terrific - it was Joe who had become the wreck.

Three Main Reasons for Nonfiling

No matter how bad your situation has become, there's undoubtedly others who are or have been in a similar or worse nonfiling situation.

For the most part, I have found that there are three prime reasons that people fail to file tax returns; financial difficulties, procrastination, and actual tax protestors.

Financial Difficulties

Through the years, I've found that male nonfilers outnumber females approximately four to one, the main reason being divorce. However, if you look at the group as a whole it is usually because people, regardless of gender, have run into financial difficulties - whether this be the result of a divorce, loss of a job, a failing business, or bankruptcy. Usually there is also some emotional turmoil attached. A death in the family, divorce, business failures and bankruptcies can cause depression, despondency, and tremendous amounts of emotional pressure as well as financial. When people find themselves in financial difficulty coupled with emotional stress, they may decide not to file their tax returns.

Case Study:
John works for a large company as a computer salesman. He has been married for ten years and has two children. In June of 1988, however, John moves out of the marital home and files for divorce.

8 • Failure To File

As is typical with men, John does not fare well financially with the divorce. He is left with his clothes, an automobile, a boat, and hefty alimony and child support payments. John's income is $50,000 per year and his wife was not working at the time of divorce. If we take a look at John's new tax situation, it looks something like this:

Changes in John's 1988 Tax Status

	Married Filed Jointly		**Single**
Gross Income	$50,000		$50,000
Item. Deduction	($18,000)	Standard Deduction	($ 3,000)
Exemptions (4)	($ 8,000)	(1)	($ 2,000)
Taxable Income	$24,000		$45,000
Federal Income Tax	$ 4,793		$10,380
Tax Increase of	$5,587		

In the past, John usually received small refunds. As you can see by the illustration, however, his taxes have increased by $5,587, and he won't be at all prepared for this. He won't even think to change his W4 at work from married to single. John's real mistake is that he doesn't do anything about his situation - probably because he is terribly preoccupied emotionally with the divorce.

The court orders John to pay child support and alimony payments of $1,200 per month, which is another $14,400 per year, leaving him with far less cash flow than he's accustomed. In addition, he has car payments of $400 per month and a boat payment of the same amount. Also, John must set up house. He will need a new place to live and many household items. In fact, he could probably use about half of everything that K-mart sells; from towels, drapes, pots, and pans, to furniture, television, and coffee maker. He's running up his credit cards, too, just to make ends meet. Eventually, John will also want to start dating again, hoping to take his date to more than a fast-food restaurant. Life has suddenly become terribly expensive.

There is also an important emotional factor present in situations comparable to John's. Because of the way the current judicial system operates (no matter what the reason for divorce) men usually end up with next to nothing coming out of a divorce, leaving them with an implied feeling that they are to blame for the failed relationship. This often results in depression and an "I don't give a damn" attitude, feeling stepped on by the world and betrayed by the court system. On April 15, John realizes he has a tax liability that he is unable to pay. Faced with such a tough financial situation he decides not to file his tax returns just in order to survive.

John's case is really quite typical, but there is a light at the end of the tunnel. We'll revisit John in Chapter 8.

Procrastinators

Probably of anything we are required to do by our federal government, filing income tax returns is by far the worst annual inconvenience that we will go through, and the highest expense of our lifetime. Things like voter registration, renewing licenses, and even signing up for the draft are minor league when compared to filing income tax returns and the possible consequences of failing to do so.

First of all, there is a huge amount of paperwork required. Even if you are using a tax professional, there are still organizational materials to go through in order to prepare records properly. It is a time consuming and unpleasant requirement imposed on us by our government, so it's easy to understand why 7 to 10 percent of the population fails to make the April 15th deadline and end up having to file extensions.

Consider, though, that *one third* of all nonfilers (again, that number is in the 10 to 15 million range) have refunds coming, so financial difficulty is not always the question here. Sometimes, it's simply a case of procrastination.

Case Study:

Steve was retired from General Motors, where he had worked for 40 years and was receiving a pension. Steve was married, owned his own home and had itemized deductions consisting of real estate taxes, mortgage interest and charitable contributions. Steve would have been entitled to refunds during each of the last three years, had he simply filed his income tax returns.

During this three year period, Steve received the standard statutory notices from the Internal Revenue. In fact, he was inundated with IRS correspondence, but he never responded to even one piece of mail. Finally, the IRS estimated his income tax and sent him a 30 day letter (calculating his taxes), followed by a 90 day letter assessing his tax liability. After receiving the 90 day letter, Steve waited 85 days before he finally showed up at my office.

Naturally, the Government based their assessment on a worst case scenario. They had calculated Steve's returns as married filing separately with no deductions. Had Steve waited the full 90 days, this "inflated" tax assessment would have been final. He would have had absolutely no recourse. Actually, Steve's returns should have been filed married/jointly with itemized deductions, resulting in small refunds. (See illustration.)

Steve's Income Tax Summary

Married Filing Jointly				**Married Filing Separately**		
1990	1991	1992		1990	1991	1992

Taxable Income

1990	1991	1992		1990	1991	1992
$25,000	$25,000	$25,000		$25,000	$25,000	$25,000

Tax

$3,754	$3,754	$3,754		$4,898	$4,797	$4,604

Tax Withheld

$4,000	$4,000	$4,000		$4,000	$4,000	$4,000

Refund				**Liability**		
$ 246	$ 246	$ 246		($ 898)	($ 797)	($ 604)

Total refund over three years, $738

12 • FAILURE TO FILE

Approximate interest and penalties:	($ 546)	($ 487)	($ 444)
	($1444)	($1284)	($1048)
	======	======	======

Total tax liability with interest and penalties for three year period: $3,776, making a difference of $4,514
=====   =====

As you can see by the illustration, (even based on a fairly modest retirement income), the final results are rather dramatic. In Steve's particular case, there is an actual difference in tax liability of $4,514. If this situation hadn't been so serious, it could have been funny. After all, Steve was retired, so it wasn't as if he'd been too busy to file his taxes on a timely basis, or even too busy to respond to the IRS letters and readily resolve the problem. Certainly, having financial or emotional difficulties can cause people to procrastinate filing their income tax returns. In Steve's case, however, neither financial difficulties nor emotional turmoil were factors in his failing to file the returns. It all boiled down to simple procrastination.

Tax Protestors

The two groups outlined above comprise about 98% of all nonfilers. The remaining 2% is a very small group, albeit a very vocal one. They are deliberate tax protestors.

It is not the intention of this book to support tax protestors in any way. I believe everyone should join in and pay their share of taxes for two very important reasons. First of all, it takes an incredible amount of money to run a country. Our whole economic system of survival as a country is based on the collection of taxes and all are required to help shoulder that burden.

Secondly, it's the law. For this reason, I have to believe that trying to take on the U.S. government is borderline suicidal. A lone individual trying to tackle the United States Government seems comparable to the suicide mission of Saddam Hussein; at least Hussein had a military of sorts to back him up.

To most tax protestors, their refusal to pay taxes has very little to do with monetary reasons. To them, it's a matter of principle. If you are a tax protestor, you probably have very serious, staunch convictions on the subject and feel very justified in your actions (or non-action in this case). You probably feel theoretically correct in your arguments and have pieced together bodies of law that seem to support your stance. But there is one serious flaw in your plan - you aren't as powerful as the U.S. Government.

Saddam Hussein Syndrome

Case Study:
Bill was a skilled automotive draftsman for a firm in Madison Heights, Michigan, making about $20 an hour in prototype design. He had a family, owned two cars and enjoyed a modest life-style; pretty much the average American. Between 1981 and 1986 Bill made nearly a quarter of a million dollars - but he never paid one cent in taxes. Bill had come to believe that he didn't owe any taxes, so he simply quit filing.

During the early 1980's, there were a lot of unemployed people in Michigan who had a lot of time to get together and talk about things like taxes. In fact, the early eighties produced one of the largest tax revolts in U.S. history. "We the People ACT (American Citizens Tribunal)" originated when a group of some 7,500 auto workers in the Pontiac and Flint areas decided to fill out withholding tax forms to reflect 99 exemption or tax exempt status. Doing either of the two would prevent their employers from withholding taxes from their pay. In a nut shell, they believed that if everyone followed suit, the Government could not possibly throw everyone in jail.

Though Bill has distanced himself from any affiliation with this extreme group, he still admits to having attended anti-tax meetings and came to believe that skilled wages were not taxable as income. He asserted that wages were merely compensation for the work done by your brain or skill and not an income, which is a return on capital. He contended that taxes on sales and services are legal, but taxes on wages violate an individual's rights and are unconstitutional. Interestingly, his points have legal merit.

In 1981, Bill decided to act on what he believed and stopped filing his income tax returns. In 1988 he still held fast to his convictions, even though the government had thrown him in federal prison for a two year term plus a $2,000 fine for nonfiling. At that time, his tax liability was estimated at around $71,000, plus interest and penalties. However, after serving his prison term and still refusing to file his returns, Bill now owes the government almost $400,000.

Bill came into my office in 1992 after his release from prison. He has filed his current taxes, but still hasn't decided whether or not to file his past taxes. It seems this is still a matter of principle to him, even though he seems a broken man, completely ravaged by the system. Bill does not have the means to pay his tax liability and I have advised him to file his returns and then, after three years from that assessment date, file for bankruptcy. (Three years is the bankruptcy time statute that will enable us to include taxes as dischargeable.) Still, Bill seems hesitant.

I have found that the determining factor in getting a tax protestor back on track with the IRS is whether the individual has the *desire* to settle up with the government *before* they are charged criminally.

If you are a tax protestor, you have very little chance of beating the IRS. Consider that once you are caught and tried, you will be facing a judge whose wages are paid out of the federal withholding system and the jury will probably be stocked with teachers and government workers of some sort, and probably all of them will be current regarding their taxes. Therefore, no matter how well-constructed your case may be, you probably won't be receiving too much sympathy from anyone.

You could possibly admire someone like Bill for at least standing up for what he believes in. Nonetheless, it is a losing battle and the tax protestor will probably not only end up spending some time in prison, but will also owe the monies anyway with huge interest and penalties besides.

Odds in Favor of the IRS

One important note regarding filing back returns is that if you owe the federal government for any number of past years, you still owe - no matter how far back you go. But if you have refunds coming for past years you will only be able to collect *the last three years in refunds.* For example, if you filed a 1990 tax return in April 1991, the three years you could receive the refund would take you to 1994. After that, you cannot collect on the refund. Likewise, any refunds you would have been entitled to prior to the 1990 tax year will be forfeited by April 15th 1994.

I know. But fair has nothing to do with it.

*"Let me tell you how it will be
one for you, nineteen for me."
    - From the song "Tax Man"
    by the Beatles*

2

Getting With The Program

No matter how it may feel at times, you are not alone in your nonfiling predicament. The IRS estimates there are 10 million nonfilers in this country, but I believe that number to be closer to 15 million because of the self-employed who work mainly for cash - a large group of people who have gone undetected by the IRS for years. These people are operating in a kind of "underground" economy.

A great number of nonfilers have learned to get by in this society with no credit cards, mortgages, checking accounts or car loans - however, there are many exceptions. I recently consulted a client who had not filed his income tax returns in 12 years, having *never* been contacted by the IRS. He was a self-employed cabinet maker, owned a home, had a land contract, had credit cards, a checking account and had even financed a vehicle - all without catching the watchful eye of the Government.

Consider also that these estimated 15 million plus nonfilers have stunted the budget by approximately $10 billion annually in delinquent taxes. It's no surprise, therefore, that in October 1992 the Government implemented a nonfiler program in order to recoup this massive loss to the budget. What *is* surprising is that they waited so long to do something about it.

Perhaps the reason the IRS waited so long to "reel in" nonfilers was manpower constraints. During the 1980's, most agents were kept incredibly busy examining tax shelters. But, since the 1986 tax act, most of these shelters have disappeared. Also, until computerization it was extremely time-consuming, costly, and difficult to track the elusive paper trail of the delinquent taxpayer. Even with these considerations, though, it is interesting to note that (prior to this nonfiling program) the IRS seemingly ignored those who failed to even *file* tax returns and instead opted to concentrate on the millions of Americans who faithfully prepared and submitted their tax returns, only to be audited by rather fussy agents.

How the Program Works (Knowing Your Enemy)

As part of the nonfiler program, the IRS has allocated a staff of almost 2,300 (about 20% of their field agents) for an estimated two year period. This program will probably make a dent in the number of nonfiling cases, but every year another couple of million people drop off the system (by becoming nonfilers) so this is an on-going problem for the IRS.

The field auditors assigned to the nonfiler program are typically a group of auditors that were handling large 1040's or auditing partnership and corporate income tax returns. In terms of the IRS, these auditors are among the most sophisticated of their staff. In speaking with many of these agents, it is my understanding that this program was designed to begin with the lower income people and work its way up the income scale. Therefore, if you are a nonfiler that has not as yet been contacted by the IRS, this doesn't necessarily mean you have been overlooked - it simply means your "number" hasn't as yet been called.

Also, even though this particular program was designed to run for only two years doesn't mean the IRS will simply forget about addressing the nonfiler dilemma. What probably will happen is that once the program is completed, the IRS will be more strict and more cases will be turned over to the criminal division for prosecution.

Locating the Nonfiler

100% Matching Process

How does the IRS find the nonfiling taxpayer? Through their 100% matching process. Every year, the IRS matches W2's, 1099's, and other income-oriented documents to filed income tax returns. If no match is found, a correspondence campaign begins.

The IRS has a fairly archaic computer system. Certainly if they possessed today's technology, the IRS could very well locate practically *every* nonfiler. It is very hard for Congress to approve the millions of dollars it would take to modernize the system, though. It's not politically popular because it has such a "big brother" sound to it. But it is feasible to think that one day, in the near future, the IRS will have the capability of matching such things as checking accounts, credit information and buying habits to income tax returns.

Reward

Another way the IRS discovers nonfilers is when someone turns them in. The IRS offers a reward of 10% of the "base" tax (the actual tax liability excluding interest and penalties) to the person who reports a nonfiler.

Initial Contact

Once the IRS has located a nonfiling individual, they try to make contact by letter - if the taxpayer doesn't respond, they send a series of letters. This happens prior to a field agent being assigned to the case. I have clients who received as many as fifty or more letters before actual, personal contact by an agent. Even though each letter becomes increasingly adamant in tone, sometimes the IRS still fails to prod the taxpayer into responding. (See illustrations.)

The Ten Day Letter

If after a period of time you fail to respond to the IRS, a field agent might call or visit your home or place of employment. If the agent is still unable to make personal contact with you, he or she may leave a business card or - as a last

Getting With The Program • 23

Department of the Treasury
Internal Revenue Service

If you have any questions, refer to this information:
Date of This Notice:
Taxpayer Identifying Number:
  Form   Tax Year Ended   Document Locator
  1040   Number

|..|..||..|.|||.|||.|||.|.|....|..||..|.|.||.|.|.|||...||||.|

Call:

or

Write: Chief, Taxpayer Assistance Section
Internal Revenue Service Center

If you write, be sure to attach the bottom part of this notice.

REMINDER OF UNPAID TAX

THE FEDERAL TAX SHOWN BELOW HAS NOT BEEN PAID. IT IS OVERDUE. PLEASE PAY IT TODAY.

MAKE YOUR CHECK OR MONEY ORDER PAYABLE TO INTERNAL REVENUE SERVICE. WRITE YOUR TAXPAYER IDENTIFYING NUMBER ON YOUR PAYMENT. RETURN THE BOTTOM PART OF THIS NOTICE WITH YOUR PAYMENT IN THE ENCLOSED ENVELOPE. IF YOU BELIEVE THIS BILL IS INCORRECT, SEND THE AMOUNT YOU THINK IS DUE AND EXPLAIN THE DIFFERENCE.

THE ENCLOSED PUBLICATION 1 PROVIDES IMPORTANT INFORMATION ABOUT YOUR RIGHTS AS A TAXPAYER. PLEASE KEEP FOR FUTURE REFERENCE.

WE HAVE CALCULATED PENALTY AND INTEREST TO THE DATE OF THIS NOTICE. IF YOUR PAYMENT IS NOT RECEIVED WITHIN 10 DAYS FROM THE DATE OF THIS NOTICE, ADDITIONAL PENALTIES AND INTEREST MAY BE CHARGED.

TAX FORM NUMBER   1040
TAX PERIOD ENDED

BALANCE OF PRIOR ASSESSMENTS
LATE PAYMENT PENALTY
INTEREST

TOTAL AMOUNT DUE

ENCLOSURES:
ENVELOPE
PUBLICATION 1

If you have any questions, you may call or write -- see the information in the upper right corner of this notice. To make sure IRS employees give courteous responses and correct information to taxpayers, a second employee sometimes listens in on telephone calls.
See back of this notice for more information.
Keep this part for your records.   ↓ DETACH HERE ↓   Form 8125 (Rev 4-86)

24 • Failure To File

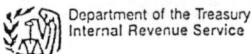 Department of the Treasury
Internal Revenue Service

IF YOU HAVE ANY QUESTIONS, refer to this information:
NUMBER OF THIS NOTICE:
DATE OF THIS NOTICE:
TAXPAYER IDENTIFICATION NUMBER:
FORM:
TAX PERIOD:

For assistance call:

or use the address below.

HAVE YOU FILED YOUR TAX RETURN?

ALTHOUGH WE HAVE PREVIOUSLY ASKED YOU TO FILE YOUR FORM 1040 , US INDIVIDUAL INCOME TAX RETURN , FOR THE TAX PERIOD ENDING 12-31-90, WE HAVE NOT HEARD FROM YOU.

IF YOU HAVE NOT FILED THIS TAX RETURN, DO SO TODAY. BE SURE TO ATTACH YOUR PAYMENT FOR ANY TAX DUE. IF YOU CAN'T PAY THE ENTIRE AMOUNT OF TAX YOU OWE NOW, SEND AS LARGE A PAYMENT AS YOU CAN AND TELL US WHEN YOU CAN PAY THE REST. WE MAY BE ABLE TO ARRANGE FOR YOU TO PAY IN INSTALLMENTS.

IF YOU FILED THIS TAX RETURN WITHIN THE LAST 6 WEEKS, PLEASE DISREGARD THIS NOTICE.

UNDER THE LAW, WILLFULLY FAILING TO FILE A TAX RETURN CAN RESULT IN FINES, CRIMINAL PENALTIES, OR BOTH. TO PREVENT THESE ACTIONS, YOU SHOULD FILE YOUR TAX RETURN TODAY.

IF YOU THINK YOU ARE NOT REQUIRED TO FILE, PLEASE TELL US WHY BY COMPLETING THE INFORMATION THAT APPLIES TO YOU ON THE ENCLOSED FORM 9358, "INFORMATION ABOUT YOUR TAX RETURN."

BE SURE TO DETACH AND INCLUDE THE BOTTOM PART OF THIS NOTICE IN THE ENCLOSED ENVELOPE WHEN YOU SEND US YOUR TAX RETURN OR THE COMPLETED FORM 9358.

Getting With The Program • 25

Department of the Treasury
Internal Revenue Service

If you have any questions, refer to this information:
Date of This Notice:
Taxpayer Identifying Number:
    Form   Tax Year Ended   Document Locator Number
    1040

Call:

or

Write: Chief, Taxpayer Assistance Section
         Internal Revenue Service Center

If you write, be sure to attach the bottom part of this notice.

OVERDUE TAX

WE HAVE PREVIOUSLY WRITTEN TO YOU ABOUT THE FEDERAL TAX SHOWN BELOW. ADDITIONAL INTEREST AND PENALTIES ARE INCLUDED. PLEASE PAY IT NOW.

SEND FULL PAYMENT BY CHECK OR MONEY ORDER PAYABLE TO THE INTERNAL REVENUE SERVICE. WRITE YOUR TAXPAYER IDENTIFICATION NUMBER ON YOUR PAYMENT. INCLUDE THE BOTTOM PART OF THIS NOTICE WITH YOUR PAYMENT SO WE CAN QUICKLY IDENTIFY AND CREDIT YOUR ACCOUNT.

IF YOU THINK THIS BILL IS INCORRECT, SEND THE AMOUNT YOU BELIEVE IS DUE AND EXPLAIN THE DIFFERENCE. IF PAYMENTS HAVE NOT BEEN CREDITED TO YOUR ACCOUNT, FOLLOW THE INSTRUCTIONS ON THE BACK OF THIS NOTICE.

WE HAVE CALCULATED PENALTY AND INTEREST TO THE DATE OF THIS NOTICE. IF YOUR PAYMENT IS NOT RECEIVED WITHIN 10 DAYS FROM THE DATE OF THIS NOTICE, ADDITIONAL PENALTIES AND INTEREST MAY BE CHARGED.

TAX FORM NUMBER   1040
TAX PERIOD ENDED

BALANCE OF PRIOR ASSESSMENTS
LATE PAYMENT PENALTY
INTEREST

TOTAL AMOUNT DUE

ENCLOSURES:
ENVELOPE

If you have any questions, you may call or write -- see the information in the upper right corner of this notice. To make sure IRS employees give courteous responses and correct information to taxpayers, a second employee sometimes listens in on telephone calls.
See back of this notice for more information.
Keep this part for your records.   ↓ DETACH HERE ↓   Form 8125 (Rev 4-86)

26 • Failure To File

Department of the Treasury
Internal Revenue Service

If you have any questions, refer to this information:
Date of This Notice:
Taxpayer Identifying Number:
    Form   Tax Year Ended   Document Locator Number
    1040

Call:

or

Write: Chief, Taxpayer Assistance Section
         Internal Revenue Service Center

If you write, be sure to attach the bottom part of this notice.

URGENT - PAYMENT REQUIRED

YOUR FULL PAYMENT OF THE FEDERAL TAX SHOWN BELOW HAS STILL NOT BEEN RECEIVED. WE HAVE PREVIOUSLY BILLED YOU FOR THE OVERDUE TAX AND MUST NOW CONSIDER FILING A NOTICE OF FEDERAL TAX LIEN AND SEIZING YOUR PROPERTY, WAGES, OR OTHER ASSETS TO SATISFY YOUR UNPAID TAX. THE AMOUNT DUE INCLUDES ADDITIONAL INTEREST AND PENALTIES WHICH WILL CONTINUE TO INCREASE UNTIL THE BALANCE IS PAID IN FULL. WE HAVE CALCULATED PENALTY AND INTEREST TO THE DATE OF THIS NOTICE. IF YOUR PAYMENT IS NOT RECEIVED WITHIN 10 DAYS FROM THE DATE OF THIS NOTICE, ADDITIONAL PENALTIES AND INTEREST MAY BE CHARGED.

SEND FULL PAYMENT TODAY BY CHECK OR MONEY ORDER PAYABLE TO INTERNAL REVENUE SERVICE. WRITE YOUR TAXPAYER IDENTIFYING NUMBER ON YOUR PAYMENT. INCLUDE THE BOTTOM PART OF THIS NOTICE WITH YOUR PAYMENT SO WE CAN QUICKLY IDENTIFY AND CREDIT YOUR ACCOUNT.

IF YOU THINK THIS BILL IS INCORRECT, SEND THE AMOUNT YOU BELIEVE IS DUE AND EXPLAIN THE DIFFERENCE. IF PAYMENTS HAVE NOT BEEN CREDITED TO YOUR ACCOUNT, FOLLOW THE INSTRUCTIONS ON THE BACK OF THIS NOTICE.

IF YOU ARE UNABLE TO PAY IN FULL, CONTACT US IMMEDIATELY TO EXPLAIN YOUR FINANCIAL CONDITION. WE WILL REVIEW YOUR CIRCUMSTANCES TO HELP YOU DETERMINE HOW TO PAY THE AMOUNT DUE. INSTALLMENT PAYMENTS OR PAYROLL DEDUCTION MAY BE CONSIDERED.

YOUR PROMPT RESPONSE IS NECESSARY.

TAX FORM NUMBER   1040
TAX PERIOD ENDED

BALANCE OF PRIOR ASSESSMENTS
LATE PAYMENT PENALTY
INTEREST

TOTAL AMOUNT DUE

ENCLOSURES:
ENVELOPE

If you have any questions, you may call or write -- see the information in the upper right corner of this notice. To make sure IRS employees give courteous responses and correct information to taxpayers, a second employee sometimes listens in on telephone calls.
See back of this notice for more information.
Keep this part for your records.   ↓ DETACH HERE ↓   Form 8125 (Rev. 4-86)

Getting With The Program • 27

Department of the Treasury
Internal Revenue Service

DATE OF NOTICE:
TAXPAYER IDENTIFYING NUMBER:
FORM 1040   TAX PERIOD

FOR ASSISTANCE YOU MAY CALL US AT:

OR YOU MAY WRITE TO US AT THE
ADDRESS SHOWN AT THE LEFT. IF
YOU WRITE, BE SURE TO ATTACH
THE BOTTOM PART OF THIS NOTICE.

NOTICE OF INTENT TO LEVY

THIS IS YOUR FINAL NOTICE. YOUR FULL PAYMENT OF THE FEDERAL TAX SHOWN BELOW HAS STILL NOT BEEN RECEIVED. IF FULL PAYMENT IS NOT RECEIVED WITHIN TEN DAYS FROM THE DATE OF THIS NOTICE, ADDITIONAL INTEREST AND PENALTIES WILL BE CHARGED.

A NOTICE OF FEDERAL TAX LIEN MAY BE FILED, WHICH IS A PUBLIC NOTICE THAT THERE IS A TAX LIEN AGAINST YOUR PROPERTY. AS PROVIDED BY SECTION 6331 OF THE INTERNAL REVENUE CODE, YOUR PROPERTY OR RIGHTS TO PROPERTY MAY BE SEIZED. THIS INCLUDES SALARY OR WAGES, BANK ACCOUNTS, COMMISSIONS, OR OTHER INCOME. REAL ESTATE AND PERSONAL PROPERTY SUCH AS AUTOMOBILES, MAY ALSO BE SEIZED AND SOLD TO PAY YOUR TAX.

TO PREVENT THIS ACTION, SEND FULL PAYMENT TODAY BY CHECK OR MONEY ORDER PAYABLE TO INTERNAL REVENUE SERVICE. WRITE YOUR TAXPAYER IDENTIFYING NUMBER ON YOUR PAYMENT. INCLUDE THE BOTTOM PART OF THIS NOTICE WITH YOUR PAYMENT SO WE CAN QUICKLY IDENTIFY AND CREDIT YOUR ACCOUNT.

WE HAVE CALCULATED PENALTY AND INTEREST AMOUNTS TO THE DATE OF THIS NOTICE. THE FAILURE TO PAY PENALTY INCREASES FROM ONE HALF PERCENT TO ONE PERCENT PER MONTH AFTER THIS NOTICE.

IF YOU RECENTLY PAID THE AMOUNT DUE, OR IF YOU CANNOT PAY THIS AMOUNT IN FULL, CONTACT THE OFFICE SHOWN ABOVE TODAY. AS EXPLAINED IN THE ENCLOSED PUBLICATION, ENFORCEMENT ACTION MAY BE TAKEN 30 DAYS AFTER THIS NOTICE.

```
                                                               TAX FORM:  1040
                                                               TAX PERIOD:
BALANCE OF PRIOR ASSESSMENTS
LATE PAYMENT PENALTY
INTEREST

TOTAL AMOUNT DUE
```

TO MAKE SURE IRS EMPLOYEES GIVE COURTEOUS RESPONSES AND CORRECT INFORMATION TO TAXPAYERS, A SECOND EMPLOYEE SOMETIMES LISTENS IN ON TELEPHONE CALLS.
KEEP THIS PART FOR YOUR RECORDS   FORM 8126 (Rev. 9-88)

effort - issue a 10 day letter (see illustration). This letter states that if the taxpayer doesn't respond within ten days the IRS will estimate their tax (which, of course, will be based on a worst case scenario.)

The Thirty Day Letter

The calculated tax which the IRS prepares is outlined in a 30 day letter and mailed to you, notifying you of what your estimated tax will be (see illustration). The IRS will not be kind or generous in their estimation, but rather base the tax liability on a worst case scenario.

If you do not respond to or dispute the proposed tax as outlined in the 30 day letter, the IRS will send a 90 day letter in which the tax is actually assessed.

The Ninety Day Letter

When the IRS has grown weary of its letter-writing campaign, they may decide to put together your tax return based on whatever information they have. Again, the IRS will base your tax liability on a worst case scenario (without proper deductions/exemptions, i.e. an "inflated" tax).

Up until a 90 day letter, the IRS has simply wanted you to file your tax returns. In the event of a 90 day letter, though, the matter will no longer be between you and the IRS. Rather, after the 90 day period has elapsed, things will then be between you and the collection division. (See Chapter 6 for more on collections.)

INTERNAL REVENUE SERVICE   DEPARTMENT OF THE TREASURY

DISTRICT DIRECTOR

                                PERSON TO CONTACT:

                                TELEPHONE NUMBER:

                                REFER REPLY TO:

                                DATE: November 12, 1993

Dear

I have been assigned the investigation of your failure to file your
individual Federal income tax returns for the years 1987, 1988, 1989, 1990
1991, and 1992.

I prefer that you voluntarily file your returns within 10 days of the date
on this letter. If you wish to file these returns please mail them to the
address listed above and to the attention of   If you have a
problem meeting this deadline contact me at   If you owe money with
these returns please submit payment. If you are unable to pay in full at this
time, we can arrange a payment schedule.

Some of these cases will result in criminal prosecutions; however, no
taxpayer who was not already under investigation has ever been criminally
prosecuted if he or she came forward and made a full, honest and complete
disclosure about non-filing, and then filed the returns due.

If you have any questions, please call me at the number noted above.

                        Sincerely,

30 • Failure To File

DEPARTMENT OF THE TREASURY

CINCINNATI SERVICE CENTER
P.O. BOX 145500   STOP 812
CINCINNATI, OH   45214

DATE:

INTERNAL REVENUE SERVICE
PROPOSED INDIVIDUAL INCOME TAX ASSESSMENT

SOCIAL SECURITY NUMBER:

TAX YEAR:
PERSON TO CONTACT:
TAX TECHNICIAN -
CONTACT TELEPHONE NUMBER:

OFFICE HOURS:

DEAR

WE HAVE NO RECORD OF RECEIVING YOUR FORM 1040, U.S. INDIVIDUAL INCOME TAX RETURN, FOR THE TAX YEAR SHOWN ABOVE. WE HAVE COMPUTED YOUR TAX, PENALTIES, AND INTEREST BASED ON INCOME REPORTED TO US BY YOUR EMPLOYER(S), BANK(S), ETC., AS SHOWN ON PAGE 5. PAGE 2 SHOWS OUR TAX COMPUTATION. THIS COMPUTATION DOES NOT GIVE YOU FULL CREDIT FOR EXEMPTIONS, DEDUCTIONS OR CREDITS.

YOUR BEST COURSE OF ACTION IS TO FILE YOUR OWN TAX RETURN(S) NOW TO CLAIM YOUR CREDITS AS PROVIDED BY LAW.

YOU HAVE 30 DAYS FROM THE DATE OF THIS LETTER TO COMPLETE ONE OF THE FOLLOWING:

1. FILE YOUR FORM 1040 AND ATTACH THE ENCLOSED NOTICE 949 TO IT;
2. SIGN AND DATE THE "CONSENT TO ASSESSMENT AND COLLECTION" FORM ON PAGE 4 AND RETURN IT TO US IN THE ENCLOSED ENVELOPE;
3. EXPLAIN WHY YOU ARE NOT REQUIRED TO FILE OR ENCLOSE INFORMATION YOU WOULD LIKE US TO CONSIDER; OR
4. APPEAL THE PROPOSED ASSESSMENT. ENCLOSED ARE PUBLICATION 5, "APPEAL RIGHTS AND PREPARATION OF PROTESTS FOR UNAGREED CASES," AND PUBLICATION 1 "YOUR RIGHTS AS A TAXPAYER," EXPLAINING THE RIGHTS YOU HAVE CONCERNING ASSESSMENT AND PAYMENT OF TAX.

IF YOU CANNOT PAY ALL THE TAX, SEND AS MUCH AS YOU CAN, AND TELL US WHEN YOU CAN PAY THE REST. WE MAY BE ABLE TO ARRANGE FOR YOU TO PAY THE BALANCE IN INSTALLMENTS, PROVIDED ALL YOUR TAX RETURNS ARE FILED.

IF YOU DO NOT RESPOND WITHIN 30 DAYS, WE WILL PROCEED WITH THE ASSESSMENT OF TAX AND PENALTIES BASED ON OUR COMPUTATIONS.

YOU MAY ORDER BLANK TAX FORMS, SCHEDULES, INSTRUCTIONS, AND PUBLICATIONS BY CALLING TOLL FREE   ONCE YOU HAVE PLACED YOUR ORDER, ALLOW TWO WEEKS FOR DELIVERY.

IF YOU HAVE QUESTIONS, WRITE OR CALL THE PERSON WHOSE NAME AND NUMBER ARE SHOWN ABOVE. IF YOU WRITE, PROVIDE YOUR TELEPHONE NUMBER AND MOST CONVENIENT TIME FOR US TO CALL, IF NECESSARY. PLEASE ATTACH PAGE 1 OF THIS LETTER TO YOUR REPLY AND USE THE ENCLOSED ENVELOPE.

                                        SINCERELY,

                                        CHIEF, COLLECTION BRANCH

ENCLOSURES:
PUBLICATIONS 1 & 5
NOTICES 433, 609, & 949
RETURN ENVELOPE

PAGE 1   LETTER 2566SC/CG (REV. 6/91)

Getting With The Program • 31

Department of the Treasury
Internal Revenue Service
CINCINNATI, OH 45214   P 913 765 891

1774200000 ASFR

Date:
MAY 19, 1993

Tax Year Ended and Deficiency:
DEC. 31, 1988 *****5,058.00

Person to Contact:
TAX TECHNICIAN   -   SFR

Contact Telephone Number:
606-292-5055
Between 7:30 AM and 3:30 PM
(Not a toll free number)

STEPHEN M DONOVAN
%JAMES E JENKINS C P A
17288 WEST 12 MILE ROAD
SOUTHFIELD, MI 48076

362-54-7219

Dear Taxpayer:

We have determined that there is a deficiency (increase) in your income tax as shown above. This letter is a NOTICE OF DEFICIENCY sent to you as required by law. The enclosed statement shows how we figured the deficiency.

If you want to contest this deficiency in court before making any payment, you have 90 days from the above mailing date of this letter (150 days if addressed to you outside of the United States) to file a petition with the United States Tax Court for a redetermination of the deficiency. The petition should be filed with the United States Tax Court, 400 Second Street NW, Washington, D.C. 20217, and the copy of this letter should be attached to the petition. The time in which you must file a petition with the Court (90 or 150 days as the case may be) is fixed by law and the Court cannot consider your case if your petition is filed late. If this letter is addressed to both a husband and wife, and both want to petition the Tax Court, both must sign the petition or each must file a separate, signed petition.

If you dispute not more than $10,000 for any one tax year, a simplified procedure is provided by the Tax Court for small tax cases. You can obtain information about this procedure, as well as a petition form you can use, by writing to the Clerk of the United States Tax Court at 400 Second Street NW., Washington, D.C. 20217. You should do this promptly if you intend to file a petition with the Tax Court.

If you decide not to file a petition with the Tax Court, we would appreciate it if you would sign and return the enclosed waiver form. This will permit us to assess the deficiency quickly and will limit the accumulation of interest. The enclosed envelope is for your convenience. If you decide not to sign and return the statement and you do not timely petition the Tax Court, the law requires us to assess and bill you for the deficiency after 90 days from the above mailing date of this letter (150 days if this letter is addressed to you outside the United States).

If you have any questions about this letter, please write to the person whose name and address are shown above, or you may call that person at the number shown above. If this number is outside your local calling area, there will be a long distance charge to you. If you prefer, you may call the IRS telephone number listed in your local directory. An IRS employee there will be able to help you, but the office at the address shown on this letter is most familiar with your case.

When you send the information we requested or if you write to us with questions about this letter, please provide your telephone number and the most convenient time for us to call if we need additional information. Please attach this letter to any correspondence to help us identify your case. Keep the copy for your records.

Thank you for your cooperation.

Sincerely yours,

Commissioner
By

Frederic P. Williams
Director, Service Center

Enclosures:
Copy of this letter
Waiver
Envelope

Form 5601 (Rev. 4-85)

The 90 day letter will be sent to you in the form of a bill. What really gives this letter teeth is that along with this tax assessment is a letter stating that if you do not file a tax court petition (see Chapter 4) disputing the tax within 90 days, you will simply owe the money with *no recourse*. The tax assessment will be engraved in stone. Certainly, there *may* be recourse if you can prove that you never received the 90 day letter (for instance, you were held hostage in Iran), but you will need to come up with a very convincing reason. Neither the IRS or the tax courts are very lenient in this area.

Collectable Liability

The purpose of the 90 day letter is to establish a *collectable liability* on the part of the IRS. Because a 90 day letter notifies a taxpayer of their tax liability which is coupled with a direct demand of such payment, if no payment is made, the IRS has the legal right to levy wages, file liens and/or garnishee bank accounts in order to collect on this debt. These are strong-arm tactics used by the IRS in order to force the filing of your tax returns.

A particularly effective method of forcing the returns is with a lien or levy (see Chapter 4 for more on lien and levy). For example, a favorite tactic of the IRS is to place a levy on an individual's wages. There is a standard exemption of $75.00 exemption per pay period, plus $25.00 per exemption. However, due to other deductions from your paycheck, you could be left with far less. I've seen individuals left with as little as $8.70 per week. Any attempt to lift a levy is useless until you file your income tax returns.

The Summons Power

Probably one of the strongest weapons the IRS has in its powerful, government-backed arsenal is the *power to summon information* (see illustration). For seemingly arbitrary reasons, some IRS agents bypass the 30 day and 90 day letter process and go straight to issuing a summons. This is usually done when the IRS feels they do not have enough income information to properly assess taxes (via a 90 day letter) and they believe the tax liability to be substantial.

The IRS generally doesn't need a court order to demand this information. Consequently, it is a fairly easy procedure for an agent who is seeking information to force you to bring your income documents or prepared returns to an IRS office - usually within a 30 day period after receiving the summons. If the summons is ignored and you fail to produce the tax information requested, the IRS will contact the FBI or Federal Marshals who will have you arrested and placed in jail until such time as it takes for your lawyer to bail you out.

Usually, the IRS does not issue a summons unless they have run out of patience with a taxpayer who keeps putting them off. It is an effective whip to get an individual moving. If you have already received a summons, the IRS is very serious. They are done playing the stalling game and it's probably a good time to consider professional tax help.

However, if the IRS has not as yet issued a summons but they are pushing you to produce financial information or completed tax returns by a certain date, it is important to note that these "requests" are not contractual in any way. Certainly, it is advisable to work with the IRS and keep your relationship

34 • FAILURE TO FILE

Form 2039
(Rev. July 1992)

Summons

Department of the Treasury
Internal Revenue Service

In the matter of _____

Internal Revenue District of _____ Periods _____

The Commissioner of Internal Revenue

To _____

At _____

You are hereby summoned and required to appear before _____ ___
an officer of the Internal Revenue Service, to give testimony and to bring with you and to produce for examination the following books, records, papers, and other data relating to the tax liability or the collection of the tax liability or for the purpose of inquiring into any offense connected with the administration or enforcement of the internal revenue laws concerning the person identified above for the periods shown.

DO NOT WRITE IN THIS SPACE

Business address and telephone number of Internal Revenue Service officer named above:

_____

Place and time for appearance:

at _____

on the _____ day of _____, 19____ at _____ o'clock ___m.

Issued under authority of the Internal Revenue Code this ____ day of _____, 19____

_____   _____
Signature of Issuing Officer   Title

_____   _____
Signature of Approving Officer (if applicable)   Title

Original to be kept by IRS

Form 2039 (Rev. 7-92)

10/19/92   Published by Tax Management Inc., a Subsidiary of The Bureau of National Affairs, Inc.   2039.1

Getting With The Program • 35

Service of Summons, Notice and Recordkeeper Certificates

(Pursuant to section 7603, Internal Revenue Code)

I certify that I served the summons shown on the front of this form on:

Date	Time

How Summons Was Served

☐ I handed an attested copy of the summons to the person to whom it was directed.

_____

_____

☐ I left an attested copy of the summons at the last and usual place of abode of the person to whom it was directed. I left the copy with the following person (if any):

_____

_____

Signature	Title

This certificate is made to show compliance with section 7609, Internal Revenue Code. This certificate applies only to summonses served on third-party recordkeepers and not to summonses served on other third parties or any officer or employee of the person to whose liability the summons relates nor to summonses issued in aid of collection, to determine the identity of a person having a numbered account or similar arrangement, or to determine whether or not records of the business transactions or affairs of an identified person have been made or kept.

I certify that, within 3 days of serving the summons, I gave notice (Form 2039-D) to the person named below on the date and in the manner indicated.

Date of Giving Notice _____ Time: _____

Name of Noticee: _____

Address of Noticee (if mailed): _____

How Notice Was Given

☐ I gave notice by certified or registered mail to the last known address of the noticee.

☐ In the absence of a last known address of the noticee, I left the notice with the person summoned.

☐ I gave notice by handing it to the noticee.

☐ I left the notice at the last and usual place of abode of the noticee. I left the copy with the following person (if any).

☐ No notice is required.

Signature	Title

I certify that the period prescribed for beginning a proceeding to quash this summons has expired and that no such proceeding was instituted or that the noticee consents to the examination.

Signature	Title

Form 2039 (Rev. 7-92)

2039.2   Published by Tax Management Inc., a Subsidiary of The Bureau of National Affairs, Inc.   10/19/92

36 • FAILURE TO FILE

Form 2039
(Rev. July 1992)

Summons

Department of the Treasury
Internal Revenue Service

In the matter of _____

Internal Revenue District of _____ Periods _____

The Commissioner of Internal Revenue

To _____

At _____

You are hereby summoned and required to appear before _____
an officer of the Internal Revenue Service, to give testimony and to bring with you and to produce for examination the following books, records, papers, and other data relating to the tax liability or the collection of the tax liability or for the purpose of inquiring into any offense connected with the administration or enforcement of the internal revenue laws concerning the person identified above for the periods shown.

_____

"I hereby certify that I have examined and compared this copy of the summons with the original and that it is a true and correct copy of the original."

_____   _____
Signature of IRS Official Serving the Summons   Title

Business address and telephone number of Internal Revenue Service officer named above:

_____

Place and time for appearance:

at _____

on the _____ day of _____, 19____ at _____ o'clock ___m.

Issued under authority of the Internal Revenue Code this ____ day of _____, 19____

_____   _____
Signature of Issuing Officer   Title

_____   _____
Signature of Approving Officer (if applicable)   Title

Part A — To be given to person summoned   Form 2039 (Rev. 7-92)

10/19/92   Published by Tax Management Inc., a Subsidiary of The Bureau of National Affairs, Inc.   2039.3

with them running as smoothly as possible. However, until the summons is actually issued, these demands are simply strong requests and you are not necessarily bound to comply.

Criminal Intent

Finally, and most importantly, whether you have received any of the above IRS correspondence or not, it is imperative that you contact the IRS. This is best done by letter. An "intent to file" letter will remove from you any suggestion of criminal intent. In other words, the letter will be evidence that you are aware of your nonfiling status and that you are not attempting to avoid the payment of these taxes.

The letter should be similar to the following:

Ima Taxpayer
Anytown, USA

Re: Social Security #

Dear Madam or Sir:

I have not filed my income tax returns for the following year(s) (list the year(s). I intend to file these returns as soon as possible. I am currently gathering information in order to file the returns in the near future.

If you have any questions, please call me at

Sincerely,

Ima Taxpayer

"There is no art which one government sooner learns of another than that of draining money from the pockets of the people."
  - Samuel Smiles

3

The Importance Of An Overall Strategy

EVEN IF YOUR current situation with the IRS is pretty tense, it is imperative to take the time to develop an overall strategy *prior to filing your income tax returns.* This is extremely important because once you file the returns you will be "locked in" to a position. Every option must be explored. Any type of tactical financial maneuvers must be accomplished prior to filing your returns or you will have lost much of your positioning power.

Also, prior to filing the returns, you will have the advantage over the IRS because you will know much more than they at this point - especially if you haven't as yet been contacted by the IRS but rather decided to address this situation of your own volition. Once you file the returns, though, the IRS will have the advantage because they will know your tax status and can begin collection procedures. During collection, everything will be on *their* terms.

To Hire, or Not to Hire

One of the first questions to ask yourself is if you will employ a tax professional to prepare your tax returns and/or represent you, or if you will be handling this matter yourself. You may not know the answer to this question until you have read further into this book. I should say now, though, that if you have received a ninety day letter or a summons from the IRS, I strongly suggest you employ a tax professional. However, it will be extremely beneficial for you to read this book in its entirety whether employing a tax professional, or not, since you will be the one affected by the outcome.

Employing a Tax Professional

If you decide to use a tax professional, you should always remember that *you* are the captain of the ship. You are the general, and the tax practitioners, attorneys, etc. are merely hired troops. They will (hopefully) be well-trained, nevertheless they will be working *for* you. It is not wise to leave the decision of decisive action, direction or tactics solely to the troops. Certainly, part of their job will be to advise and inform you. But remember that you will reap the harvest or havoc of what occurs.

Therefore, it is important to choose capable, well-seasoned troops, i.e. a tax practitioner who is experienced and competent. First of all, interview a tax professional. You don't have to stay with the first person you approach. Choose a tax practitioner that you feel comfortable working with; one who is (or at least seems) sympathetic toward your nonfiling situation. If they show disregard or a judgmental attitude toward your nonfiling predicament, it's probably a good idea to move on to the next candidate. (This, too, will depend on how much pressure you're receiving from the IRS. You may not have the time to shop around.)

Secondly, you will need a tax professional who is familiar with all the aspects that I will outline in this book. A tax practitioner's edition of this book is available and recommended for the tax professional that you employ. Tell your tax practitioner that they can obtain a copy of this book by calling 1-800-345-0096 and that you strongly recommend it.

Also, my practice (Jenkins & Company), handles cases nationally and you can contact my staff in Southfield, Michigan. We would be willing to talk to you on a one-time basis as a free consultation. In addition, when you obtained a copy of this book, you became entitled to a free call to our Tax Research Service with any nonfiling question (see Chapter 9).

If you do decide to employ a tax professional, don't simply leave everything up to them. Read this book in its entirety and take an active part in developing your strategy. Professionals make mistakes, too. By keeping yourself informed you will be less likely to suffer consequences that could have been avoided.

Going it Alone

Whether you have decided on hiring a tax professional or not, you will need to read this book carefully and in its entirety. If you have decided against employing a tax professional, you will need to employ some or all of the outlined strategies and tactics contained within this book in order to deal effectively with the IRS. While this book may not be tailored to every question or unique dilemma, it is quite comprehensive.

Should you decide to handle this matter on your own, you should remember one important thing: do not ever let an IRS agent intimidate you. Most of these agents are very good at what they do. They are masters of intimidation and of asking leading questions. By all means, attempt to stay on good terms with the IRS, but don't let an agent railroad you into or out of anything.

Also, if it is not your desire to prepare the returns (and since this book is not an instruction booklet on how to fill out and file tax returns) it may be a good idea to employ a tax practitioner for this purpose. Then, use this book to gauge your tax professional's performance (remember, they are just hired troops) and employ the asset-protecting strategies and insights contained herein.

Assessing the Damage

You've had a chance to sit down, relax, take a deep breath and recover somewhat from the anxiety of nonfiling. Now it's time to roll up your shirt sleeves and get to work.

The first step to correcting or fixing a problem is to properly assess the damage. Developing an overall strategy can only be done effectively by assessing not only your *tax status*, but also *financial status*, and determining the *extent of IRS action (if any) thus far*.

Tax Status

You will need to come up with at least an approximation of what your tax debt will be. Ask yourself certain questions.: How long has it been since you filed your returns? To what kind of deductions and exemptions are you entitled? This doesn't have to be a concrete number, but it will be important to know whether the tax liability will be within your means to pay off, or if it has ballooned to an unmanageable size. For instance, quite often the interest and penalties can nearly double your tax liability.

Financial Status

The only way to know whether you have the ability to handle the estimated tax liability will be to determine your current financial status. Your ability to pay off the debt will have much to do with whether you have a steady income or a fluctuating, commission-based income.

Be realistic. Too many times people are far too optimistic when assessing their financial status. Even if you are in a higher income bracket, it can still be difficult to make payments because you are locked into more financial commitments. You may think you can afford to pay $500 per month toward your tax liability, when in actuality, you may only be able to afford $100 or $200 per month and still maintain a good standard of living.

Ask yourself these questions: What are your assets and liabilities? Can you manage a strict payment arrangement with the IRS, coupled with a severe decrease in spendable income as you pay your tax debt? Remember, once you file your tax returns and begin to make payment on your taxes, you will also need to stay current with paying current taxes, so your income will be reduced two-fold; one, by the possible payment arrangement you may enter into with the IRS to pay off your past tax liability, and two, setting aside monies currently for next year's filing of tax returns. Because of this, you could very well see your monthly budget reduced by as much as 50%. Also, you will need to take into consideration unexpected expenses that often arise. So, try to be realistic when assessing your financial status and ability to pay off your tax debt. (See Chapter 8 on bankruptcy options.)

Extent of IRS Contact or Action

The last step that will affect your overall strategy (actually, in great measure) is the extent of IRS contact thus far.

If the initial letter-writing campaign is still in progress, it will be enough to simply respond to the IRS, letting them know your nonfiling situation is not being ignored. In fact, this would be a good time to inform the IRS that the situation is being addressed at the current time and you will be filing your returns shortly (once you get all of your income and deduction documents pieced together). This should satisfy them for a period of time and may alleviate further tension and also hopefully prevent (or at least postpone) some of the more adamant letters (10 day, 30 day, 90 day), especially a possible summons.

If, however, you have already received a 30 day or 90 day letter, you will need to act very quickly, as this puts a definite time table on the process. If this is the case, I strongly recommend employing a tax professional, even if your tax liability is not substantial.

These three factors will greatly determine the course you take regarding an overall strategy. The extent of IRS contact in particular will play a major role in setting the pace for accomplishing the end goal - the actual filing of the tax returns.

Understanding Statutes

There are two statutes that will also affect the pace and direction in which you will proceed with your overall plan. Throughout this book are examples and further explanations of these statutes, but at least a cursory knowledge of them is paramount at this time.

Ten Year Statute of Limitations

The Revenue Reconciliation Act of 1990 extended the six year statute of limitations to ten years for the collection of taxes. This statute allows the IRS to take collection action against a taxpayer for a period of ten years. This statute begins on the assessment date of the taxes (usually the date the taxes were filed). During this ten year period, the IRS must either enforce collection through administrative collection (levy, seizure) or institute a suit for collection of the taxpayer's unpaid federal tax liability (initiate a judicial collection proceeding).

Sometimes the IRS will try to "blackmail" a taxpayer into extending this statute to fifteen or twenty years by threatening to place levies or liens on property, bank accounts, or wages, unless you agree to extend the statute, thereby allowing the IRS more time to collect the full liability.

Bankruptcy Statute

In bankruptcy, taxes are a *priority item*. This means that, generally speaking, taxes cannot be discharged in Chapter 7 bankruptcy. However, your tax debt *can* be discharged in bankruptcy if the petition is filed after three years have passed from the tax assessment date. Also, under Chapter 7 bankruptcy, if you file the petition before your tax debt has passed this three year mark, even though the "base tax" debt would not be discharged, the interest and penalties *would* be dischargeable, thereby greatly reducing your tax liability in most cases. (See Chapter 8 for more on bankruptcy.)

Preparation

Part of your overall strategy will be concerning the preparation of the returns (even though you will have some asset-protecting maneuvers to accomplish prior to filing). Buying time with the IRS can reduce stress significantly. Gathering necessary income information can be time consuming and frustrating simply because of the number of years that may be involved, and missing information can stop you dead in your tracks when you want or need to move forward.

Buying Time

Stalling for time is often a necessity in nonfiling cases. It is advantageous to have the most time possible to assess the damage, decide on an overall strategy, work out a financial analysis, collect and sift through information, determine your tax liability, prepare the returns, and try to delay a payment arrangement until a more convenient time. Buying time can be accomplished several ways.

First of all, if you are having difficulty obtaining necessary income information from outside sources, relay this to the agent assigned to your case. Be explicit. Explain to the agent in great detail, the problems you are experiencing in gathering the needed information. State the exact documents you are missing; W2, 1099, real estate taxes, mortgage interest, bank interest. Relate to the agent that you have requested certain pieces of information from various third parties and they have not responded as quickly as you had anticipated. Blaming the postal service also works well; it buys time and also properly documents the process. For example, don't request income information from banks or employers by telephone. Write letters requesting this information. This can buy you weeks of time.

You can also blame IRS red tape. Who knows better than an IRS agent just how long it takes for the system to respond to inquiries. If you need more income information to piece together your tax liability, you can order this information directly from the IRS. Use Form 4506 (see illustration) which can be obtained at an IRS office near you. It usually takes 8 to 12 weeks for a response and should elicit a more understanding response from your agent. But NEVER tell an agent that you are too busy to work on the returns.

I can not stress enough how important it will be, regarding all of the tactics you will be using, to never come across as a hard nose or uncooperative with the IRS in any form or manner. Blaming someone else, like the bank, past employers,

48 • FAILURE TO FILE

Form **4506**
(Rev. August 1992)
Department of the Treasury
Internal Revenue Service

Request for Copy of Tax Form

▶ Please read instructions before completing this form.
▶ Please type or print clearly.

OMB No. 1545-0429
Expires 6-30-95

Note: *Do not use this form to get tax account information. Instead, see instructions below.*

1a Your name shown on tax form	1b Your social security number or employer identification number. (See instructions.)
2a If a joint return, spouse's name shown on tax form	2b Spouse's social security number

3 Current name and address (including apt., room, or suite no.)

4 If copy of form is to be mailed to someone else, show the third party's name and address. (See instructions.)

5 If we cannot find a record of your tax form and you want the payment refunded to the third party, check here . . . . . ▶ ☐
6 If name in third party's records differs from line 1a above, show name here. (See instructions.)

7 Check the box to show what you want:
  a ☐ Copy of tax form and all attachments (including Form(s) W-2, schedules, or other forms). The charge is $4.25 for each period requested.
     Note: *If these copies must be certified for court or administrative proceedings, see instructions and check here* . . . . . ▶ ☐
  b ☐ Copy of Form(s) W-2 only. There is no charge for this. See instructions for when Form W-2 is available.

8 Tax form number (Form 1040, 1040A, 941, etc.)

10 Amount due for copy of tax form:	
a Cost for each period	$ 4.25
b Number of tax periods requested on line 9	
c Total cost. Multiply line 10a by line 10b.	$

9 Tax period(s) (year or period ended date). If more than four, see instructions.

Full payment must accompany your request. Make check or money order payable to "Internal Revenue Service."

Please Sign Here
Signature. See instructions. If other than taxpayer, attach authorization document.   Date
Title (if line 1a above is a corporation, partnership, estate, or trust)

Telephone number of requester ( )
Convenient time for us to call

Instructions

Purpose of Form.—Use Form 4506 only to get a copy of a tax form or Form W-2. But if you need a copy of your Form(s) W-2 for social security purposes only, do not use this form. Instead, contact your local Social Security Administration office.

Do not use this form to request Forms 1099. Copies of Forms 1099 are not available from the IRS. If you need a copy of a 1099 form, contact the payer. Also, **do not** use this form to request tax account information.

Note: *If you had your tax form filled in by a paid preparer, check first to see if you can get a copy from the preparer. This may save you both time and money.*

Please allow at least 45 days for delivery. To avoid any delay, be sure to furnish all the information asked for on this form. You must allow 6 weeks processing time after a tax form is filed before requesting a copy.

Tax Account Information Only.—A listing of certain tax account information is available free of charge if you write or visit an IRS office or call the IRS toll-free number listed in your telephone directory.

Generally, tax account information is needed when students applying for financial aid are required to give the college a copy of their tax form. The school may, however, accept tax account information provided by the IRS instead. If so, the following information will be sent upon request:

• Name and social security number.
• Type of return filed.
• Filing status.
• Tax shown on return.
• Adjusted gross income.
• Taxable income.
• Self-employment tax.
• Number of exemptions.
• Amount of refund.
• Amount of earned income credit.

Mortgage Revenue Bonds.—States issuing mortgage revenue bonds are required to verify that the mortgage applicant did not own a home during the 3 previous years. As part of this verification, the mortgage lender may want proof that you did not claim interest or real estate tax deductions for a residence on your tax return. If you have a copy of your tax return, or if it was filled out by a paid preparer and you can get a copy, the mortgage lender can accept your signed copy.

If you filed Form 1040A or 1040EZ, you can request tax account information to help satisfy the verification requirement. To do this, **do not** complete this form. Instead, contact your local IRS office for this information.

If you filed Form 1040, you may have to get a copy of it to verify that you did not claim any itemized deductions for a residence. To get a copy, **complete** Form 4506 and write "Mortgage Revenue Bond" across the top.

Line 1b.—Enter your employer identification number **only** if you are requesting a copy of a **business** tax form. Otherwise, enter your social security number shown on the tax form.

(Continued on back)

For Paperwork Reduction Act Notice, see back of form.   Cat. No. 41721E   Form **4506** (Rev. 8-92)

4506.1

The Importance Of An Overall Strategy • 49

Form 4506 (Rev. 8-92)   Page 2

Line 2b.—If requesting a joint tax form, enter your spouse's social security number.

Note: *If you do not complete line 1b and, if applicable, line 2b, there may be a delay in processing your request.*

Line 4.—If you have named someone else to receive the tax form (such as a CPA, an enrolled agent, a scholarship board, or a mortgage lender), enter the name of an individual and the address to ensure the copy gets to the right person. If we cannot fill your request and you want the payment for copies refunded to the third party, check the box on line 5.

Line 6.—Enter the name of the client, student, or applicant if it is different from the name shown on line 1a. For example, the name on line 1a may be the parent of a student applying for financial aid. In this case, you would enter the student's name on line 6 so the scholarship board can associate the tax form with their file. If we cannot find a record of your tax form, we will notify the third party directly that we cannot fill the request.

Line 7a.—If you are requesting a certified copy of a tax form for court or administrative proceedings, check this box. It will take at least 60 days to process your request.

Line 7b.—If you need only a copy of your Form(s) W-2, check this box. Also, on line 8 enter "Form(s) W-2 only" and on line 10c enter "no charge."

If your address on line 3 is different from the address shown on the last return you filed and you haven't filed **Form 8822,** Change of Address, or otherwise notified the IRS in writing of your new address, you must attach either—

• A copy of two pieces of identification that have your signature, or

• An original notarized statement affirming your identity.

Form W-2 is not available until 6 weeks after you file it with your tax return (for example, Form 1040). Otherwise, Form W-2 information is only available 18 months after it is submitted by your employer. If you lost your Form W-2 or have not received it by the time you are ready to prepare your tax return, contact your employer.

Line 9.—Enter the year(s) of the tax form you are requesting. For fiscal-year filers or requests for quarterly tax forms, enter the date the period ended; for example, 3/31/89, 6/30/89, etc., for a quarterly filed tax form. If you need more than four different tax periods, use additional Forms 4506. Tax forms that were filed 6 or more years ago may not be available for making copies. However, tax account information is generally still available for these periods. See **Tax Account Information Only** on page 1.

Line 10c.—Write your social security number or Federal employer identification number and "Form 4506 Request" on your check or money order. If we cannot fill your request, we will refund your payment.

Signature.—Requests for copies of tax forms to be sent to a third party must be signed by the person whose name is shown on line 1a, unless the third party has your authorization (discussed later) to receive the copies.

Copies of jointly filed tax forms may be furnished to either the husband or the wife. Only one signature is required. Sign Form 4506 exactly as your name appeared on the original tax form. If you changed your name, also sign your current name.

For a corporation, the signature of the president of the corporation, or any principal officer and the secretary, or the principal officer and another officer are generally required. For more details on who may obtain tax information on corporations, partnerships, estates, and trusts, see Internal Revenue Code section 6103.

If you are not the taxpayer shown on line 1a, you must attach your authorization to receive a copy of the requested tax form. An authorization must specifically state what tax form and period(s) is covered and that the requested tax form(s) may be given to the person designated authority by the taxpayer. You may attach a copy of the authorization document if the original has already been filed with the IRS. This will generally be a power of attorney, or other authorization such as evidence of entitlement (for Title 11 Bankruptcy or Receivership Proceedings). If the taxpayer is deceased, you must send Letters Testamentary or other evidence to establish that you are authorized to act for the taxpayer's estate.

Note: *Form 4506 must be received by the IRS within 60 days after the date you signed and dated the request.*

Where To File.—Mail Form 4506 with the correct total payment attached to the **Internal Revenue Service Center** for the place where you lived when the requested tax form was filed.

Note: *You must use a separate form for each service center from which you are requesting a copy of your tax form.*

If you lived in: **Use this address:**

If you lived in:	Use this address:
New Jersey, New York (New York City and counties of Nassau, Rockland, Suffolk, and Westchester)	1040 Waverly Ave. Stop 532 Holtsville, NY 11742
New York (all other counties), Connecticut, Maine, Massachusetts, New Hampshire, Rhode Island, Vermont	310 Lowell St. Stop 679 Andover, MA 01810
Florida, Georgia, South Carolina	P.O. Box 47-412 Photocopy Unit Stop 91 Doraville, GA 30362
Indiana, Kentucky, Michigan, Ohio, West Virginia	P.O. Box 145500 Cincinnati, OH 45250-5500
Kansas, New Mexico, Oklahoma, Texas	3651 South Interregional Highway Photocopy Unit Stop 6716 Austin, TX 73301

Alaska, Arizona, California (counties of Alpine, Amador, Butte, Calaveras, Colusa, Contra Costa, Del Norte, El Dorado, Glenn, Humboldt, Lake, Lassen, Marin, Mendocino, Modoc, Napa, Nevada, Placer, Plumas, Sacramento, San Joaquin, Shasta, Sierra, Siskiyou, Solano, Sonoma, Sutter, Tehama, Trinity, Yolo, and Yuba), Colorado, Idaho, Montana, Nebraska, Nevada, North Dakota, Oregon, South Dakota, Utah, Washington, Wyoming	P.O. Box 9953 TPR/Photocopy C6 Mail Stop 6734 Ogden, UT 84409
California (all other counties), Hawaii	5045 E. Butler Avenue Photocopy Unit Stop 52350 Fresno, CA 93888
Illinois, Iowa, Minnesota, Missouri, Wisconsin	2306 E. Bannister Road Annex 1, Bldg. 41 Photocopy Unit Stop 57 Kansas City, MO 64131
Alabama, Arkansas, Louisiana, Mississippi, North Carolina, Tennessee,	P.O. Box 2501 Stop 46 Memphis, TN 38101
Delaware, District of Columbia, Maryland, Pennsylvania, Virginia, a Foreign country, or had an A.P.O. or F.P.O address	P.O. Box 920 Photocopy Unit Drop Point 536 Bensalem, PA 19020

Privacy Act and Paperwork Reduction Act Notice.—We ask for the information on this form to carry out the Internal Revenue laws of the United States. We need it to gain access to your tax form in our files and properly respond to your request. If you do not furnish the information, we may not be able to fill your request.

The time needed to complete and file this form will vary depending on individual circumstances. The estimated average time is:

Recordkeeping	13 min.
Learning about the law or the form	7 min.
Preparing the form	21 min.
Copying, assembling, and sending the form to the IRS	17 min.

If you have comments concerning the accuracy of these time estimates or suggestions for making this form more simple, we would be happy to hear from you. You can write to both the **Internal Revenue Service,** Washington, DC 20224, Attention: IRS Reports Clearance Officer, T:FP; and the **Office of Management and Budget,** Paperwork Reduction Project (1545-0429), Washington, DC 20503. **DO NOT** send this form to either of these offices. Instead, see **Where To File** on this page.

4506.2   Published by Tax Management Inc., a Subsidiary of The Bureau of National Affairs, Inc.   10/19/92

or even IRS red tape certainly helps. Even risk appearing absent-minded, if need be. But never appear uncooperative or resistant in any way, no matter how much an agent may tempt you. Buying time will help you greatly in developing an overall strategy and in gathering necessary information. However, it is important to keep in mind the two time statutes outlined above. Buying time is beneficial in terms of putting together the tax returns. However, remember that the statutes do not begin until the actual filing of the income tax returns. This "time factor" regarding your overall strategy can be crucial.

Gathering Information

When lacking necessary information, a basic starting point will be the last tax return you filed. If you are not able to produce a copy of this return, it can be obtained from the IRS by filing form 4506 (see illustration) which can be obtained from your local IRS office.

A *tax organizer* may be appropriate for some nonfiling situations. This is a lengthy form, but rather simple. It can help a great deal when attempting to piece together your tax puzzle (see illustration).

Because there are often multiple years involved in most nonfiling cases, it is often difficult to produce accurate documentation, i.e. incomplete documentation. In order to complete the returns you may need to use estimates. For example, if you are self-employed and unable to establish income, you may have to resort to bank records. If there are missing bank records, you may have to resort to standard of living calculations. These are acceptable methods recognized by the

IRS. In fact, if the IRS were calculating returns for you, they would use these same exact methods to establish income in the event of missing information. It's better that you put together this information than leaving it to the IRS.

Case Study:

In the 1960's, Alan served in Viet Nam. After the war, he became addicted to drugs in the 1970's, then kicked his drug habit and worked as a self-employed carpenter. During this entire time he never paid or filed income taxes. Though he was never contacted by the IRS, he voluntarily came into my office wishing to get on track with his taxes.

One of the first questions I ask any nonfiler is the last time they filed taxes, so I asked Alan this question. He didn't respond. In fact, he completely changed the subject. After hearing him out, I pressed him again for an answer. Still no response. For a third time I pressed very hard for a response to when he last filed his income tax. Alan looked me square in the eye and said, "I understand the question, Jim. I just don't have the answer." It had been so long, he could not remember the last time he'd filed. In fact, we even had trouble coming up with the approximate decade he had stopped filing. We could only guess. Therefore, we simply went back six years.

Explanation: If you haven't filed your taxes in a number of years, an IRS collection procedural manual suggests that agents limit their inquiry to six years. This doesn't mean, however, that the IRS won't go ahead and assess a tax debt for periods longer than six years if they have substantial income documents to support the liability.

52 • FAILURE TO FILE

Topic Index   1

Topic Index	Form
Alimony paid or received	11
Annuity payments received	9, 11
Auto information:	
Business	5A
Employee business expense	16
Farm	10A
Rent and royalty	8A
Business income and expenses	5
Business use of home	5B, 10B
Child and dependent care expenses	17
Contributions	14
Dependent information	3
Depreciable property and equipment:	
Business	5
Employee business expense	16
Farm	10
Rent and royalty	8
Dividend income	4
Electronic filing request	19
Employee business expense	16
Estate income	9
Estate taxes	15
Estimated taxes	18
Farm income and expenses	10
Foreign dividend income	4B
Foreign employment information	3A, 3B
Foreign interest income	4A
Foreign taxes	3D
Foreign wages and other income	3C

Topic Index	Form
Installment sale receipts	6
Interest income	4
Interest paid	13
Investment interest expense	13
IRA contributions	12
IRA distributions	11
Keogh plan contributions	12
Medical and dental expense	13
Miscellaneous income and adjustments	11
Miscellaneous itemized deductions	15
Mortgage interest	13
Moving expenses	7
Partnership income	9
Pension payments received	9, 11
Personal information	3
Railroad retirement benefits	11
REMICs	9
Rent and royalty income and expenses	8
S corporation income	9
Sale of personal residence	7
Sale of stock, securities, and other capital assets	6
SEP plan contributions	12
Social security benefits	11
State and local tax refunds	11
Taxes paid	13
Tax preparation fee	15
Trust income	9
Unemployment compensation	11
Wages and salaries	3

Organizer Legend

Throughout the tax organizer you will find columns with the heading "TSJ" or "STATE".

    TSJ Codes – Enter "T" if the indicated item is for the taxpayer, enter "S" if the indicated item is for the spouse, or enter "J" if the indicated item is joint.

    State Code – Use this area to identify the state, using state postal abbreviation, if the indicated item did not occur in your resident state.

301011 08-11-93

The Importance Of An Overall Strategy • 53

Questions — 2

If any of the following items pertain to you or your spouse for the year 1993, please check the appropriate box and include all pertinent details.

	Yes	No

Personal Information
- Did your marital status change during 1993?
- Did your address change during 1993?
- Can you or your spouse be claimed as a dependent by another taxpayer?

Dependents
- Were there any changes in dependents from the prior year?
- Do you have any children under age 14 with unearned income more than $1000?

Purchases, Sales and Debt
- Did you have any debts cancelled, forgiven, or refinanced during 1993?
- Did you start a new business, purchase a new rental property or farm, or acquire any new interest in any partnership or S corporation during 1993?
- Did you sell, exchange, or purchase any real estate in 1993?
- Did you receive grants of stock options from your employer, exercise any stock options granted to you, or dispose of any stock acquired under a qualified employee stock purchase plan?
- Did you take out a home equity loan in 1993?
- Are you claiming a deduction for mortgage interest paid to a financial institution for which someone else received the Form 1098?
- Did you sell an existing business, rental property, farm, or any existing interest in a partnership or S corporation during 1993?

Itemized Deductions
- Did you contribute property (other than cash) with a fair market value of more than $5,000 to a charity?
- Did you incur any casualty or theft losses during the year?
- Did you move to a different home because of a change in the location of your job?

Miscellaneous
- Did you have any foreign income or pay any foreign taxes during 1993?
- Did you use gasoline or special fuels for purposes other than for a highway vehicle during the year?
- Did you purchase a new diesel powered vehicle or electric vehicle in 1993?
- Did you make gifts of more than $10,000 to any individual?
- Did you receive unreported tip income of $20 or more in any month of 1993?
- Did you engage in any bartering transactions?
- If you or your spouse are self-employed, are you or your spouse eligible to be covered under an employer's health plan at another job? If yes, how many months were you covered? ☐
- Did you pay health insurance that covered at least one of your dependent children?
- Were you or your spouse a grantor or transferor for a foreign trust, have an interest in or a signature or other authority over a bank account, securities account, or other financial account in a foreign country?
- Were you notified by the IRS or other taxing authority of any changes in prior year returns?

301021 08-26-93

54 • Failure To File

Personal Information, Dependents and Wages — 3

Personal Information

Y - Yes   N - No

	First Name and Initial	Last Name	Social Security Number	Presidential Election Contribution
Taxpayer			: :	
Spouse			: :	

	Occupation	Age on 12/31	X if Blind	Date Deceased Mo Da Yr	X if Dependent of Another
Taxpayer				: :	
Spouse				: :	

Present Mailing Address

|||| Street address .....
|||| City of residence ...
|||| State abbreviation ...   ZIP code   Apartment number

Dependents

|||| Name of child living with you that is claimed as a dependent on someone else's tax return ....

|||| Year or years for which a release of claim to exemption is given for a dependent child not living with you ....

|||| Federal tax regulations require children 1 year of age or older to have a social security number.

C - Dependent child living with taxpayer
O - Other dependents
N - Dependent child not living with taxpayer

XN - Dependent child not living with taxpayer and release of claim to exemption should be filed
E - Child qualifying you for earned income credit (household member, not a dependent)

Did dependent have over $2350 income?

TSJ	State	First Name, Initial and Last Name	Social Security Number	Age	Relationship	Months Lived in Your Home	X if Disabled	Y/N	Code
			: :						
			: :						
			: :						
			: :						

Wages and Salaries

Please enclose all copies of your current year Forms W-2.

TS	State	Employer Name, City, State	Federal Tax Withheld	Gross Wages	FICA Withheld	Medicare Tax Withheld	State Tax Withheld	Local Tax Withheld

Forms 1 and W-2

The Importance Of An Overall Strategy • 55

Interest and Dividend Income — 4

Interest Income | Please enclose copies of all Forms 1099-INT or other documents relating to interest received.

Other Interest Code: 1 – Qualified Educational Series EE Bonds   2 – Accountant's Use   3 – Forfeited Interest

Interest Income – Source and Address	Savings, Loans, and Banks	U.S. Bonds and Obligations	Tax Exempt Interest	Code	Other Interest	TSJ	State	Prior Year Amount

Dividend Income | Please enclose copies of all Forms 1099-DIV or other documents relating to dividends received.

NOTE: Please list all items sold during the year on Form 6.

Dividend Income – Source and Address	GROSS Dividends	Capital Gain Dividends	Nontaxable Dividends	U.S. Bond Interest from 1099-DIV	Tax Exempt Interest	TSJ	State	Prior Year GROSS Dividends Amount

Seller Financed Interest

Name and Address	SSN of Home Buyer	Current Year Amount	TSJ	State	Prior Year Amount

Withholding

Federal			State		
Taxpayer	Spouse	Joint	Taxpayer	Spouse	Joint

Form B-1   301041 09-14-93

56 • Failure To File

Business Income and Expenses — 5

| TSJ ☐ State ☐ | Employer identification number : _____ |

Business name _____
Street address _____
City, state and ZIP code _____

	Prior Year Amount	Current Year Amount
Business Income:		
Gross receipts............		
Returns and allowances.......		
Beginning inventory..........		
Merchandise purchased.......		
Cost of labor.............		
Materials and supplies........		
Other costs:		
_____		
_____		
_____		
Ending inventory...........		
Other Income:		
_____		
_____		
_____		
Business Expenses:		
Advertising..............		
Bad debts...............		
Car and truck expense.......		
Commissions and fees.......		
Employee benefit programs....		
Health insurance – proprietor...		
Insurance – Other...........		
Interest – Mortgage..........		

	Prior Year Amount	Current Year Amount
Business Expenses (Continued):		
Interest – Other............		
Legal & professional fees.....		
Office expense............		
Pension & profit-sharing plans..		
Rent – Vehicles & machinery...		
Rent – Other..............		
Repairs and maintenance.......		
Supplies.................		
Taxes and licenses..........		
Travel...................		
Meals and entertainment:		
Limited................		
Other.................		
Utilities.................		
Wages..................		
Other expenses:		
_____		
_____		
_____		
_____		
_____		
_____		
_____		
_____		

Property and Equipment

Acquisitions – Description	Date Acquired	Cost
	: :	
	: :	
	: :	

Dispositions – Description	Date Acquired	Cost	Date Sold	Selling Price
	: :		: :	
	: :		: :	
	: :		: :	

Was there any change in determining quantities, costs or valuations between opening and closing inventory?.. ☐ Yes ☐ No

Were you or your spouse involved in the operations of this business on a regular, continuous and substantial basis?... ☐ ☐

Forms C-1, C-2, C-3, D-2, DP-1, and DP-2   301051 09-15-93

Business Auto and Other Listed Property — 5A

Please answer these questions if claiming auto expense or if you used any other listed property in your business:

Listed Property
- Automobiles
- Cellular telephones
- Property that can be used for entertainment
- Property that can be used for amusement
- Certain other vehicles
- Computers
- Property that can be used for recreation

Business Name

	Yes	No
Do you have evidence to support the business use percentage claimed on listed property?	☐	☐
Is the evidence to support the business use written?	☐	☐

If you are an employer who provides vehicles for use by employees please answer the following questions:

	Yes	No
Do you maintain a written policy statement prohibiting all personal use of vehicles, including commuting, by your employees?	☐	☐
Do you maintain a written policy statement prohibiting personal use of vehicles, except commuting, by your employees?	☐	☐
Do you provide more than five vehicles to your employees?	☐	☐
Do you treat all use of vehicles by employees as personal use?	☐	☐
Do you meet the requirements concerning fleet vehicles or qualified automobile demonstration use?	☐	☐

In addition, please answer these questions only for the automobiles used in the trade or business. (If more than one car is used in the business, use more than one column.)

	Auto No.	Auto No.
Total miles driven during the year		
Total business miles driven during the year		
Total commuting miles driven during the year		

	Yes	No	Yes	No
Was the vehicle available for personal use during off-duty hours?	☐	☐	☐	☐
Is another vehicle available for personal use?	☐	☐	☐	☐
Was the vehicle used primarily by a person who owns more than five percent interest in the trade or business?	☐	☐	☐	☐

Form DP-3   301052 04-28-93

58 • Failure To File

Business Use of Home — 5B

Part of Your Home Used for Business

	Current Year	Prior Year

Area used exclusively for business ....

Total area of home ....

Total hours home used for day-care during the year ....

	Yes	No

Was home used for day-care purposes for the entire year? ....

Were improvements made to the home and/or home office since the time you began using the home for business? ....

Expenses

List those expenses which only benefit the business part of your home as direct expenses. An example of this type of expense would be the cost of painting or repairs made to the specific area or room used for business.

List those expenses required for keeping up and running your entire home as indirect expenses. An example of this type of expense would be real estate taxes.

	Direct Expenses	Prior Year Amount	Indirect Expenses	Prior Year Amount
Casualty losses				
Mortgage interest				
Real estate taxes				
Insurance				
Repairs and maintenance				
Utilities				

Other Expenses

	Direct Expenses	Prior Year Amount	Indirect Expenses	Prior Year Amount

Form M-8   301053 07-29-93

Sales of Stocks, Securities, Capital Assets & Installment Sales — 6

Gains or Losses from Sales of Stocks, Securities and Other Capital Assets

	Yes	No
Did you sell any property in 1993 for which you will receive payments in future years?	☐	☐
Did you have any debts that became uncollectable in 1993?	☐	☐
Did you have any securities which became worthless during the year?	☐	☐
Did you have any commodity sales, short sales or straddles?	☐	☐
Did you sell any stock or stock options at a loss and then buy similar stock or options within 30 days of the sale?	☐	☐
Did you have any mutual fund transactions during the year?	☐	☐
Did you exchange any securities or investments for something other than cash?	☐	☐

Please enclose all Forms 1099-B and 1099-S.

TSJ	State	Kind of Property and Description	Date Acquired Mo Da Yr	Date Sold Mo Da Yr	Gross Sales Price (Less Commissions)	Cost or Other Basis	Federal Tax Withheld

Installment Sales

TSJ	State	Property Description	Date Sold Mo Da Yr	Principal Received	Prior Year Amount

Forms D-1, D-4, D-5, and D-10

60 • FAILURE TO FILE

Miscellaneous Income, Adjustments and Alimony —— 11

Miscellaneous Income and Adjustments

TSJ ☐ State ☐   TSJ ☐ State ☐

	Current Year Amount	Prior Year Amount	Current Year Amount	Prior Year Amount
State income tax refund				
Local income tax refund				
Taxable pensions and annuities received				
Federal withholding on pensions and annuities .				
State withholding on pensions and annuities . . .				
Unemployment compensation received				
Unemployment compensation repaid in 1993 . .				
Social security benefits received				
Social security benefits repaid in 1993				
Tier 1 railroad retirement benefits received . . .				
Tier 1 railroad retirement benefits repaid in 1993				
Lump sum taxable social security				
Taxable IRA distributions				
Nontaxable IRA distributions				
Federal withholding (Form 1099-Misc).				

Other Income

Nature and Source	Current Year Amount	TSJ	State	Prior Year Amount

Other Adjustments

Nature and Source	Current Year Amount	TSJ	State	Prior Year Amount

Alimony Paid or Received

Recipient Name	Recipient's Social Security No.	X if Alimony Received	Current Year Amount	TSJ	State	Prior Year Amount
	: :					
	: :					
	: :					

Form M-1   301111 09-17-93

The Importance Of An Overall Strategy • 61

IRA, Keogh and SEP Contributions — 12

Individual Retirement Account Information

Are you or your spouse covered by an employer's retirement plan? ☐ Yes ☐ No

	Taxpayer	Spouse
Do you want to limit your IRA contribution to the maximum amount deductible on your tax return?..............	☐ Yes ☐ No	☐ Yes ☐ No
If you answered "No" to the above question, do you want to contribute the maximum allowable amount to your IRA even though you may not qualify for an IRA deduction?..............	☐ ☐	☐ ☐
Did you receive a distribution from your IRA this year?..............	☐ ☐	☐ ☐
Did you use your IRA as security for a loan this year?..............	☐ ☐	☐ ☐

Individual Retirement Account Contributions

	Taxpayer	Spouse
Contributions made in 1993 for use on your 1993 return.............	_____	_____
Contributions made in 1994 for use on your 1993 return.............	_____	_____
Contributions for 1993 you choose to be treated as nondeductible.......	_____	_____

IRA Values, Outstanding Rollovers and Distributions

Please provide the following information if:
1) You received IRA distributions in 1993 and you have at any time made nondeductible contributions to any of your IRA(s) or:
2) You choose to make nondeductible contributions to your IRA(s) for 1993

	Taxpayer	Spouse
Value of all your IRA's on December 31, 1993.............	_____	_____
Outstanding rollovers at December 31, 1993.............	_____	_____
IRA distributions received during 1993 (Please attach Form 1099-R)......	_____	_____

Self-Employed Retirement Plan Information

	Taxpayer	Spouse
Have you established a self-employed retirement plan for which contributions are deductible?..............	☐ Yes ☐ No	☐ Yes ☐ No
Did you receive a distribution from your retirement account this year? (Please attach Form 1099-R)..............	☐ ☐	☐ ☐

TS	State	Total Amount of SEP Contributions	Defined Benefit Plan Contributions	Defined Contribution Plan Contributions	Do You Wish to Contribute the Maximum Amount to Your KEOGH?	Do You Wish to Contribute the Maximum Amount to Your SEP?
__	__	_____	_____	_____	—	—
__	__	_____	_____	_____	—	—

Forms H-1 and T-9   301121 10-05-93

Itemized Deductions - Medical, Taxes and Interest — 13

Medical and Dental Expenses

	Current Year Amount	TSJ	State	Prior Year Amount
Prescription medicines and drugs				
Total hospitalization insurance				
Total insurance reimbursement				
Number of miles traveled for medical care				
Lodging				
Doctors, dentists, etc.				
Hospitals				
Lab fees				
Eyeglasses and contacts				
Other Medical Deductions				

Taxes Paid

	Current Year Amount	TSJ	State	Prior Year Amount
Real estate taxes				
Personal property taxes				
Other Taxes Paid				

Interest Paid

Enter "X" if Form 1098 **NOT** received

	1098	Current Year Amount	TSJ	State	Prior Year Amount
Home mortgage interest paid to a financial institution					
Deductible points					

Home Mortgage Interest Paid to Individuals

To Whom Paid	Address	Social Security Number	Current Year Amount	TSJ	State	Prior Year Amount
		: :				
		: :				
		: :				

Investment Interest Expense

|||| Interest paid on money you borrowed that is allocable to property held for investment.

Description	Current Year Amount	TSJ	State	Prior Year Amount

Forms A-1 and A-2

The Importance Of An Overall Strategy • 63

Itemized Deductions - Contributions — 14

Cash Contributions

- Churches, schools, and hospitals
- Other qualified organizations and charities
- Out of pocket expenses paid in rendering services without compensation

Description of Contribution	Current Year Amount	TSJ	State	Prior Year Amount

Noncash Contributions Less Than or Equal to $500

Use this section ONLY if TOTAL noncash contributions are less than or equal to $500.

Description of Contribution	Current Year Amount	TSJ	State	Prior Year Amount

Noncash Contributions Exceeding $500

Use this section ONLY if TOTAL noncash contributions are greater than $500.

Name of donee organization _____
Address of donee organization _____

Description of Contribution	TSJ	State	Date Acquired Mo Da	Date Contributed Mo Da Yr	Cost or Basis	Fair Market Value

Method used to determine fair market value of the contribution:
Appraisal ☐   Thrift shop value ☐   Catalog ☐   Comparable sales ☐

Other method used to determine fair market value of the contribution if not marked above:
_____

How was the noncash contribution acquired:
Purchase ☐   Gift ☐   Inheritance ☐   Exchange ☐

Forms A-3, A-4 and A-5

64 • FAILURE TO FILE

Itemized Deductions - Miscellaneous — 15

Miscellaneous Itemized Deductions

	Current Year Amount	TSJ	State	Prior Year Amount
Union and professional dues				
Tax preparation fee				
Professional subscriptions				
Hobby expense (To extent of income)				
Safe deposit box				
Uniforms and protective clothing				
Work tools				
Gambling losses (To extent of winnings)				
Estate taxes				

Other Itemized Deductions

For example:
Certain legal and accounting fees
Investment expenses
Custodial fees
Employment agency fees
Certain educational expenses

Description	Current Year Amount	TSJ	State	Prior Year Amount

Form A-3   301161 08-26-93

The Importance Of An Overall Strategy • 65

Tax Payments — 18

Application of Refund

If you have an overpayment of 1993 taxes, do you want the excess:

Refunded ☐   Applied to 1994 estimated tax liability ☐

Federal Estimated Tax Payments

Please list all 1993 estimates paid	Date Due	Date Paid if After Date Due	Amount Paid
1993 1st Quarter Estimate	04-15-1993		
1993 2nd Quarter Estimate	06-15-1993		
1993 3rd Quarter Estimate	09-15-1993		
1993 4th Quarter Estimate	01-18-1994		

1992 overpayment applied to 1993 estimate...........

State and City Tax Payments

State/City _____   State/City _____

Please list all payments	Date Paid	Amount	Date Paid	Amount
Balance due paid on 1992 return				
1992 4th Quarter Estimate				
1993 1st Quarter Estimate				
1993 2nd Quarter Estimate				
1993 3rd Quarter Estimate				
1993 4th Quarter Esitmate				

1992 overpayment applied to 1993 estimate..

1994 Estimated Tax Information

	Yes	No
Do you expect a substantial change in your income for 1994?...........	☐	☐
Do you expect a substantial change in your deductions for 1994?...........	☐	☐
Do you expect a substantial change in your withholding for 1994?...........	☐	☐
Do you expect a change in the number of your dependents for 1994?...........	☐	☐
Do you expect a change in your marital status for 1994?...........	☐	☐

If You Answered "Yes" to Any of the Above Questions Please Provide Details

_____
_____
_____
_____
_____

Forms T-1, T-2, and state and city interview forms   301181 08-26-93

Missing Information

Whether you will be employing a tax professional to prepare and file your tax returns or whether you are handling this yourself, it will benefit you to know how the IRS handles missing income information. By virtue of the IRS audit guidelines, they suggest the following to agents regarding missing information:

The Internal Revenue Service has issued an Internal Revenue Manual Transmittal offering help to its examination personnel on the auditing of taxpayers under its Nonfiler Strategy. The transmittal treats such issues as selecting cases for examination, pre-contact case review, locating non-filers, examination procedures, and closing cases.

High-income nonfilers will receive the highest priority in the case selection process. Where additional information is needed to document a case file, agents are encouraged to contact employers or payors, search public records, and observe a taxpayer's personal residence. In contrast to regular audits, the Transmittal indicates that the focus of the nonfiler audit is the nonfiler's liability as a whole rather than the consideration of individual income and expense issues. The Transmittal also states that "issues should not be over-developed" and that the examiner "should rely on oral testimony and other collaborating data rather than on line-by-line documentation". The Transmittal encourages agents to refer nonfiling practitioner cases to the IRS Office of the Director of Practice.

Aggressive vs. Conservative Approach

When you don't have exact records, it is important that you document, to the best of your ability, how you are coming to your conclusions in case you are challenged by the IRS.

It's important to remember the cost/benefit relationships of the project. For example, if you are self-employed and haven't filed tax returns for 10 years, the amount of money you owe may be irrelevant since you won't be able to pay it - ever. You may as well owe the national deficit for all practical purposes. In such cases, it won't really be necessary to dig out every single expenditure since the overall picture is rather bleak. There is no point in being aggressive about the returns because you certainly don't want to find yourself in a tax fraud situation. You will probably want to assume a conservative approach in this case because (simply by virtue of nonfiling) you've already been tip-toeing in a "semi-criminal" area - no need to invite further investigation.

However, if you have had some withholding, or have perhaps paid some taxes with extensions, you may want to take a more aggressive approach regarding deductions because every dollar of tax owed becomes approximately two dollars with interest and penalties. If you can find deductions that shear down the tax liability, you will automatically be decreasing the interest and penalties.

For example, let's assume a taxpayer hasn't filed taxes between 1987 and 1992. For the first two years ('87 and '88) he owes $500 for each year, but no taxes for the last three. His $1,000 base tax liability would be closer to $2,000 with interest and penalties. As a tax professional, I would recommend this individual take a hard look at extra deductions, such as automobile deductions on Schedule C and contribution deductions on Schedule A. Such an aggressive approach may net the taxpayer a small refund, or at least (hopefully) break even.

"...Taxes upon every article which enters into the mouth, or covers the back, or is placed under the foot...taxes on everything on earth, and the waters under the earth."
  - Revd. Sydney Smith
    Review of Seybert's Statistical Annals of the United States

4

Responding To IRS Tactics

Having at least laid the basic foundation of an overall strategy, it is now important to discuss in more detail specific IRS strong-arm tactics such as the 90 day letter, penalties, lien and levy and appropriate options and responses to these tactics.

Tax Court Petition

The solution to a 90 day letter is with the tax court petition (see illustration.) The purpose of the tax court petition is to dispute the taxes as assessed by the IRS. What often occurs in my practice is that a client waits until they have a 90 day letter in hand before they come into my office asking for help.

When the process reaches this point (90 day letter), things are at a critical stage. Working with the IRS is going to be more of an uphill battle, because you will be in the completely defensive position of attempting to reduce the tax liability that the IRS has assessed. (Remember, the IRS always assumes a worst case scenario when assessing taxes. It is a case of the guilty trying to prove their innocence.)

Also, you will now be working with an IRS appeals officer who will not be treating you under typical nonfiler status any longer. The criteria seems to be much more stringent once things have progressed to a 90 day letter.

As previously stated, up until a 90 day letter, you were dealing with the IRS. However, after the 90 day letter, you will be dealing with the tax court system and a rather merciless collection division.

The only way to respond to a 90 day letter is the tax court petition, which must be filed with the completed tax returns. There is a $60.00 filing fee for each petition. A petition can cover more than one 90 day letter. Also, the petition may be filed either jointly or by a single petitioner, depending on the claim in the 90 day letter.

The completed tax court petition should be mailed to:

> United States Tax Court
> 400 Second Street, N.W.
> Washington, DC 20217

The petition can be filled out by anyone; taxpayer, CPA, accountant. However, if you are using a tax practitioner, they *cannot* file the petition for you. The petition can only be filed by you or by the lawyer who may be representing you in tax court.

As a procedural matter, your case is probably not going to end up in tax court. More often than not, you will end up meeting with an appeals officer to try and straighten out the problem. Unfortunately, what happens when you meet with an appeals officer is that a sort of mini-audit takes place. It is the officers job to prepare the case for tax court or try to resolve the matter before it ends up in court. Therefore, the agent will feel compelled to go through all of the information, receipts, and items of income. If you are attempting to handle this matter yourself (which I discourage in this type of situation) be sure that you are careful in preparing the returns and have back-up documentation and explanations because the information will be closely examined.

As already stated, you can normally get the case resolved without actually appearing in tax court. For example, in our case study of Steve (our procrastinating retiree who waited 85 days of his 90 day time limit before addressing the situation) it was simply a matter of married filing separately. The returns Steve filed were exactly the same as the IRS prepared returns, only they should have been filed married *jointly*, adding in rightful deductions and exemptions. The IRS had not taken into consideration Steve's mortgage interest or property tax deductions. These were simple, straight forward deductions. When I brought these points to the attention of the IRS agent assigned to Steve's case, we got our case wrapped up rather quickly, without ever having to go to tax court.

At other times, however, particularly with the self employed (especially when you're lacking documentation) getting the case resolved will be difficult. If you are not willing to come to a solution at this point, the case will be turned over to an attorney at the IRS. You will have another opportunity to negotiate with the IRS attorney prior to going to tax court. Actually, very few cases ever get to tax court because all you're really doing at this time (regarding the tax court petition) is filing an original return or returns and you're just trying to

74 • FAILURE TO FILE

S-36
1195:0117

FORM 2

PETITION (Small Tax Case)
(Available—Ask for Form 2)

(See Rules 170 through 179)

UNITED STATES TAX COURT

,...................................
        Petitioner(s)
              v.   } Docket No.
COMMISSIONER OF INTERNAL REVENUE,
                        Respondent

PETITION

1. Petitioner(s) disagree(s) with the tax deficiency(ies) for the year(s).........., as set forth in the NOTICE OF DEFICIENCY dated..............., 19...., A COPY OF WHICH IS ATTACHED. The notice was issued by the Office of the Internal Revenue Service at ....
                                        City   State
2. Petitioner(s)' taxpayer identification (e.g., Social Security) number(s) is (are)...
....
3. Petitioner(s) dispute(s) the following:

Year	Amount of deficiency disputed	Addition to tax (penalty), if any, disputed	Amount of overpayment claimed
.....	....	....	....
.....	....	....	....

4. Set forth those adjustments, i.e., changes, in the NOTICE OF DEFICIENCY with which you disagree and why you disagree.
....
....
....
....

Petitioner(s) request(s) that this case be conducted under the "small tax case" procedures authorized by Congress to provide the taxpayer(s) with an informal, prompt, and inexpensive hearing at a reasonably convenient location. Consistent with these objectives, a decision in a "small tax case" is final and cannot be appealed to higher Courts (the Courts of Appeals and the Supreme Court) by the Internal Revenue Service or the Petitioner(s).

....
Signature of Petitioner   Date   Present Address—Street, City, State, Zip Code, Telephone (include area code)

....
Signature of Petitioner (Spouse) Date   Present Address—Street, City, State, Zip Code, Telephone (include area code)

....
        Signature, name, address, telephone number, and Tax Court Bar Number of counsel, if retained by petitioner(s)

*If you do not want to make this request, you should place an "X" in the following box. ☐

Published by Tax Management Inc., a subsidiary of The Bureau of National Affairs, Inc.

S-36
1195:0119

FORM 4

DESIGNATION OF PLACE OF TRIAL

(Available—Ask for Form 4)

(See Rule 140)

UNITED STATES TAX COURT

.... ⎫
        Petitioner(s)   ⎬   Docket No.
             v.   ⎪
COMMISSIONER OF INTERNAL REVENUE, ⎪
                   Respondent ⎭

DESIGNATION OF PLACE OF TRIAL

Petitioner(s) hereby designate(s) .... as the place of trial of this case.   City and State

                               ....
                              Signature of Petitioner or Counsel

Dated: ...., 19....

get a properly prepared return filed. However, if you are unable to come to a mutual agreement with the appeals officer, the case will proceed into tax court, and it will be time for you to retain a competent attorney (see Chapter 8).

*Note:*The time period between the filing of the tax court petition and the trial date in tax court is usually six months.

Penalties

Sometimes individuals are surprised to find that their tax liability isn't as bad as first thought. However, with interest and penalties, the amount can quickly double. There are three, possibly four, waves of penalties. It all works in layers. First there's the underpayment of estimate penalties which will continue the entire time that the return is not filed. The penalty for failing to file a timely return, or late filing, is 5% of the tax due per month up to a maximum of 25%. Also, there's always the possibility of a negligence or disregard of rules penalties that can amount to as high as 50%.

The point is, the penalties the IRS is allowed to exact are quite severe, and the amounts add up quickly. The hierarchy is this: the actual tax, then the penalties, and then interest is charged on top of all of this. Not to mention that the interest is compounded monthly so there's interest on top of interest.

Recently, Congress has looked into this issue of IRS penalties. There has been lengthy discussion and concern raised that the IRS is allowed to exact such punitive penalties, though to date nothing has been done to change anything in terms of lessening the amounts that can be levied. Naturally, Congress is aware that these penalties are excessive, but they are hesitant to do much about them because they are a real revenue-raiser.

Another reason Congress is hesitant to remove IRS penalties is that they are an effective deterrent - ninety percent of Americans file their returns on a timely basis for fear of these penalties. However, once a taxpayer finds himself in a delinquent tax situation, the penalties actually become a deterrent to the timely collection of tax monies by the IRS. When people realize they are so far behind - not only in taxes but also in interest and penalties - they are afraid to get back on a timely tax-paying system, knowing they can't afford to pay the tax liability already owed, and the situation snowballs.

For example, if you failed to file income tax returns for five years and each year your tax was $10,000 (for a total net tax due of $50,000) the effect of the penalties on the early years would almost double the amount of the tax. So, if you owed a base tax of $50,000 over a period of five years, the actual amount owed, due to the accrual of interest and penalties, would be much closer to $80,000 or $90,000.

It's understandable why most people are not too eager to voluntarily contact the IRS and set up a payment arrangement. With penalties so severe, you can quickly get to a point of no return. In such cases, unless a person has a tremendous increase in income, hefty assets, or wins the lottery, it will be virtually impossible to pay their IRS debt.

Reality Check

Now would be a good time to address an issue raised in Chapter Three. After determining what your tax liability will be (or at least an approximation) do you have the financial ability to pay off the debt and still provide a decent existence for yourself and your family? I believe that - no matter what the tax debt - any situation is solvable; it's just not always easy. It all comes down to a simple matter of damage control. In other words, how can we settle up with the IRS leaving as much of our financial (and emotional) lives in tact as is possible?

Depending on your income and financial situation, if you haven't filed your taxes in 3 to 5 years and didn't have withholding, your tax liability may be larger than you can ever hope to pay when considering the huge amounts of interest and penalties that can accrue. True, you can set up a payment plan, but sticking to the plan may be far from easy. Consider that for every dollar of tax owed, you will probably have to match that in interest and penalties.

Also, during the years you hadn't filed, you undoubtedly became used to living *without* the payment of taxes, so your budget will tighten dramatically. For example, let's assume you have been living on $50,000 a year without paying taxes. When you file your tax returns, you will also need to get back on a tax paying system, so we can automatically subtract about $15,000 per year from your income for taxes. Also, if you enter into a payment arrangement with the IRS, paying $1,000 per month on back taxes owed, we can subtract another $12,000 per year. This will leave you with $23,000 per year spendable income when you've been accustomed to $50,000. Workable? Yes. Comfortable? Probably not.

In situations like this, bankruptcy may be a consideration (rather than trying to assume a payment plan). Chapter 8 outlines aspects and options of bankruptcy.

Waiver of Penalties

If the IRS would waive penalties, taxpayers might actually be able to pay back their tax liabilities. There are isolated cases where this is done, but I have found that the best two reasons the IRS will even *consider* waiving penalties, is in circumstances where emotional or mental disorders were a factor.

Emotional/Physical Disability

Case Study:
Neal had been a mathematics teacher for 15 years when he began to suffer some severe physical and emotional ailments and was diagnosed as a paranoid schizophrenic. Neal was forced to go on permanent disability, receiving disability payments paid out of his school district. This was a taxable disability. Neal stopped filing his income tax returns early on in his disability, which was somewhere around 1983.

Neal started receiving letters from the IRS but did nothing about them. These letters went from basically friendly reminders to not so friendly demands, and finally Neal received a 90 day letter. Neal finally brought this 90 day letter into our office, which forced us to file a tax court petition. We didn't end up going to court, but rather to the appeals division. During the examination I explained Neal's circumstances to the appeals officer and asserted that I believed there should be a full abatement of penalties due to his condition.

Of course, Neal still owed his past tax, but the appeals division decided to go along with my position and dropped all penalties and related interest - which, by the way, were substantial.

Financially Dysfunctional

Case Study:
Marie came from a very wealthy family. When her father died, he had established a trust for her that paid her approximately $70,000 per year for the rest of her life. Marie made some business ventures that failed and, despite the trust, got into some severe financial difficulties. So, in 1986 she stopped filing her income taxes.

Marie came into my office in 1990 and by then five years of returns were due. She had a lot of assets and still had the trust money coming in each year, so she was someone who was very "collectable" in terms of the IRS. We filed Marie's returns and she was, of course, charged the typical enormous penalties.

We tried to think of some way out of this for Marie. I asked her if she had at any time during the five year nonfiling period visited with a psychologist. The answer was affirmative. Then I asked her if financial matters were ever discussed with her psychologist, and the answer was also yes. With her consent, I contacted the psychologist who treated Marie and concluded that part of Marie's emotional problems were tied to financial matters. I then wrote a letter to the IRS explaining that Marie had been under psychological care and had been diagnosed as "financially dysfunctional". The IRS abated her penalties, greatly reducing her financial obligation to them.

With penalties so substantial, this can be an effective tactic to consider if it applies to your situation.

What is a Levy?

In many cases, individuals will find that they have tax assessments against them from IRS prepared tax returns. (These IRS prepared returns do not start the statute of limitations for bankruptcy). Often times, an individual is unaware of these assessments, either because he has failed to open IRS mail or has moved so many times the IRS has not caught up with him.

Generally what occurs is the IRS will place a levy against your bank or brokerage accounts. This can be done electronically. The IRS can remove or "sweep" all cash from your bank account and apply it towards your tax debt. If there is the slightest possibility of levy, you would be well-advised to withdraw all monies from your bank or securities accounts.

A levy can also be placed against your wages, leaving you with as little as $75.00 per week, plus $25.00 per exemption. I have seen instances where the amount was far less. Obviously, this places you in a very compromising position. I have found it very difficult to get a levy lifted without filing past due tax returns. This places enormous pressure on the tax professional (or yourself) in terms of getting the returns prepared. Occasionally, I have been able to get a levy released for extraordinary circumstances, such as medical problems and cases of extreme hardship. Other than an offer in compromise (more in Chapter 6) any attempt to get the levy lifted is, for the most part, useless (without filing the past due tax returns.

When the IRS is ready to release a levy, they will issue Form 668-D, Release of Levy/Release of Property from Levy (see illustration.)

Case Study:

Dennis was an employee of Ford Motor Company, steel division. Prior to that time, he worked as a self-employed salesman for a cable television company, during which time he never filed tax returns. Dennis was not very financially responsible. The IRS tried to contact him through their letter-writing campaign, but Dennis never opened even half his mail. Finally the IRS prepared the returns themselves and sent Dennis a bill for approximately $28,000, $18,000 of which was due to interest and penalties over an 8 year period.

The IRS then levied Dennis' wages - without informing him they intended to do so. Dennis got the standard $75.00 exemption, plus $25 per exemption, but had other deductions from his paycheck that were not exempt. Dennis then came into my office with a paycheck that, after deductions, totalled $8.70.

Dennis could have changed jobs, attempting to throw off the IRS wage levy, but he liked his job and it paid more than he could probably ever hope to make. All we could do was work quickly at getting his returns prepared and filed so that we could request the release of levy.

Responding To IRS Tactics • 83

Form **668-D** (Rev. April 1993)	Department of the Treasury—Internal Revenue Service **Release of Levy/Release of Property from Levy**
To	Taxpayer(s)
	Identifying Number(s)

A notice of levy was served on you and demand was made for the surrender of:

☐ all property, rights to property, money, credits and bank deposits of the taxpayer(s) named above, except as provided in 6332(c) of the Internal Revenue Code—"Special Rule For Banks." See the back of this form regarding this exception.

☐ wages, salary and other income, now owed to or becoming payable to the taxpayer(s) named above.

Please follow the instructions for the box checked below:

Release of Levy

☐ Under the provisions of Internal Revenue Code section 6343, all property, rights to property, money, credits, and bank deposits of the taxpayer(s) named above are released from the levy.

☐ Under the provisions of Internal Revenue Code section 6343, all wages, salary and other income now owed to or becoming payable to the taxpayer(s) named above are released from the levy.

Release of Property from Levy

☐ Under the provisions of Internal Revenue Code section 6343, all property, rights to property, money, credits, and bank deposits greater than $ _____ are released from the levy. The levy now attaches only to this amount.

☐ The last payment we received from you was $ _____ dated _____ . The amount the taxpayer still owes is $ _____ . When this amount is paid to the Internal Revenue Service, the levy is released. If you sent us a payment after the last payment date shown, subtract that from the amount you send now.

☐ Under the provisions of Internal Revenue Code section 6343, all wages, salary and other income ☐ **greater than** ☐ **less than** $ _____ each _____ now owed to or becoming payable to the taxpayer(s) named above are released from the levy.

Dated at _____ _____ , 19 _____ .
                    (Place)   (Date)

Signature	Telephone Number	Title

Part 3 — IRS Copy   Cat., No. 20450C   Form **668-D** (REV. 4-93)

9/20/93   Published by Tax Management Inc., a Subsidiary of The Bureau of National Affairs, Inc.   668-D.5

15

Exemptions from Levy

The following are exempt from levy:
* Clothing and school books necessary for the taxpayer and his family
* Fuel, provision, furniture, and personal effects, including firearms for his personal use, livestock, and poultry (if the taxpayer is the head of a family, the value of these items is limited to $1,650)
* Books and tools necessary for the taxpayer's business, trade or profession, provided that these items do not exceed a total value of $1,100
* Undelivered mail
* The taxpayer's principal residence (unless the District Director personally approves such levy or collection of the tax liability is in jeopardy

and
* Certain sources of the taxpayer's income, including:
(1) Unemployment benefits
(2) Certain annuity and pension payments (e.g., annuity and pension payments under the Railroad Retirement Act, benefits under the Railroad Unemployment Insurance Act, special pension payments received by a person whose name has been entered on the Army, Navy, Air Force, and Coast Guard Medal of Honor roll, and annuities based on retired or retainer pay under Chapter 73 of Title 10 of the United States Code)
(3) Workmen's compensation
(4) Judgments for support of minor children
(5) Minimum exempt amount of wages and salary

(6) Certain service-connected disability payments (i.e., amounts payable to an individual as a service-connected disability under certain provision of Title 38)

(7) Certain public assistance payments (e.g., amounts payable to a recipient of public assistance under the aid to families with dependent children (AFDC)and supplemental security income (SSI) programs or a state or local public assistance or welfare program for which eligibility is determined by a needs or income test)

(8) Assistance under the Job Training Partnership Act and

(9) Deposits to a special Treasury fund by servicemen and Public Health Service employees who are assigned to duty outside the United States.

What is a Lien?

The federal tax lien is the most widely used device of the administrative collection division of the IRS. However, a lien is merely a *security interest* and not an actual seizure of a property. Also, the lien may be subordinate to interests that third parties may have in a taxpayer's property. (See the case study of Chris and Donna under "Friendly Lien" in Chapter 5.)

In situations where nonfilers have been unknowingly assessed, the IRS typically places a general lien on the name of the individual in the county records. This may have negative effects on your credit and the ability to sell your home.

It is important to know of the existence of liens to properly analyze your strategy for filing returns and protecting assets. From a tactical standpoint, liens do not force you to file the returns, but they are most certainly an encumbrance. You can order a TRW (credit report) or call the county courthouse to find out whether a lien has been placed on your assets.

When a taxpayer fails to pay any tax for which he is liable, the IRS is given a lien against his property. It may be placed against a property after three events have taken place: 1) assessment of a tax, 2) notice and demand for the payment, and 3) nonpayment. The lien will not be released until the taxes have been paid. (See illustration for Form 668-F/Lien Release.)

Chapter Five details tactics for preventing IRS lien and possible seizure of property.

Responding To IRS Tactics • 87

Form **668-F** (Rev. December 1982)	Department of the Treasury — Internal Revenue Service **Notice of Federal Tax Lien** **Under Internal Revenue Laws**	
District	Serial number	For Optional Use by Recording Office

As provided by sections 6321, 6322, and 6323 of the Internal Revenue Code, notice is given that taxes *(including interest and penalties)* have been assessed against the following-named taxpayer. Demand for payment of this liability has been made, but it remains unpaid. Therefore, there is a lien in favor of the United States on all property and rights to property belonging to this taxpayer for the amount of these taxes, and additional penalties, interest, and costs that may accrue.

Name of taxpayer

Residence.

Kind of Tax (a)	MFT (b)	Tax Period Ended (c)	Date of Assessment (d)	Identifying Number (e)	Unpaid Balance of Assessment (f)

Place of filing

Total ▶ $

~~Chicago, IL 60602~~

Notice of Federal Tax Lien Refiling

IRS serial number _____ Recorder's identification number _____

Notice filed with _____ Date _____

Taxpayer's address *(If different than shown above)* _____

Signature _____ Title _____

This notice was prepared and signed at _____

on this the _____ day of _____, 19 _____.

Signature _____ Title _____

Note: Certificate of officer authorized by law to take acknowledgments is not essential to the validity of Notice of Federal Tax Lien G.C.M. 26419, 1950-1, C.B. 125.

Part 1 — To be kept by recording office   Form 668-F (Rev. 12-82)

"A little rebellion now and then is a good thing."
- *President Thomas Jefferson*

5

Prefiling Strategies

THERE IS ONE last step before filing, and that is to financially position yourself as favorably as possible. If there are assets to protect, bank funds to withdraw - financial tactical maneuvers of any kind - these must be done *prior* to filing your tax returns. Hindsight is everything. Once you file the returns, you're locked in.

Having read the first four chapters you have hopefully learned the usefulness of holding off filing the returns until you have a clear picture of all options available, your financial and tax status, and ability or inability to pay the tax debt. The overall objective can be summed up as follows: *The goal in a nonfiling case is not necessarily the lowest tax, but the lowest overall financial liability.* In other words, priority must be given to the protection of your assets and not necessarily the amount of the actual tax liability on the 1040. Simply put, you will need a house to live in and a car to drive after the returns are filed.

Various Filing Categories

If you are married or single and find that you have refunds coming for the past years you didn't file, simply file your returns. However, remember that if the tax assessment date is older than three years you will have forfeited the refund(s).

However, if you owe the IRS, the next few case studies will outline filing status and strategies that may help to better position you financially before filing. It will be important to read each case study carefully, because within the scenario there may be an applicable strategy for your particular tax situation.

Single/Stationary Employment

Jonathan, a divorced 32 year old, works for General Electric earning $50,000 per year. He hasn't filed his taxes since his divorce, which was five years ago, and is underwithheld. He owes the IRS $15,000 in interest and penalties.

Jonathan has assets worth protecting, especially a home he'd like to keep (see Friendly Lien on page 100 for strategies on protecting one's home).

Jonathan's goals are as follows:
1. He has an excellent job that he wants to keep.
2. He wants to continue living in his home.
3. He wants to pay back the IRS, but on his own terms.

Jonathan may consider the following strategies concerning asset protection and allocation:
1. He can have someone file a "friendly lien" on his home (see explanation of friendly lien later in this chapter).
2. Sell any stocks and bonds.
3. Remove all cash from his bank and brokerage accounts.

4. Open a bank account in someone else's name (see page 93 on levying bank accounts).
5. Purchase a new automobile or other needed items on credit.

These tactics will help accomplish three things:
1. Jonathan will have some needed items that he won't have the ability to purchase until his tax debt is paid off.
2. Reduce the amount of cash available for monthly payments to the IRS.
3. Higher debts are an advantage when filing an offer in compromise (see Chapter 7).

However, at least in Jonathan's case, an offer in compromise probably won't be seriously considered by the IRS. He is too young and the tax liability ($15,000) too small. The IRS will see the amount as fully collectible because Jonathan will be working for a number of years (not to mention earning $50,00 per year), therefore his earning power is significant.

Filing for bankruptcy (Chapter 7, or a complete liquidation) will not work in this case either. The IRS will expect to collect the tax liability (or at least most of the liability) within the three year's it would take to get past the statute of limitations whereby the tax debt would be dischargeable.

Chapter 13 bankruptcy (reorganization of debt) might offer Jonathan some relief because the payments would be spread out over a 60 month period, but the legal and court costs would make this type of move cost-prohibitive.

The one tactic that Jonathan should strongly consider is to try and reduce the related penalties. Jonathan could perhaps visit a psychologist to find out why his painful divorce drove him to financial irresponsibility (see Chapter Four, case study of Marie, Financially Dysfunctional). Using this tactic may enable Jonathan to get the penalties waived, greatly reducing his tax liability.

After the penalty issue has been resolved, Jonathan should enter into a payment arrangement with the IRS by filing Form 9465 (see Chapter Six). The last thing Jonathan should do, is get back onto a regular tax-paying system in order to avoid this problem in the future.

Single/Employed/Mobile

Karen is single. She is a computer programmer who changes her job location often, as she works on different projects, travelling throughout the United States. She has not filed her taxes in eight years and owes the IRS $87,500 including interest and penalties. Karen has no lienable assets. She owns a car but still owes money on it so the IRS isn't too interested in this asset, nor her clothes or furniture.

The average time period that Karen is employed at any one job site is six months. Remember, the IRS cannot place a levy on wages if they do not know where a taxpayer is working. It is important that Karen file her past due returns in order to establish a tax assessment date, which will also relieve her of criminal intent.

Let's assume that in April of 1993, Karen files all of her returns for the last eight years (including 1992). If she is not ready or able to enter into a payment agreement with the IRS and changes jobs in the meantime, the IRS will not be able to levy her wages as long as she does not inform them of her current place of employment. In fact, even if the IRS found out where she was working and Karen had to make payments for a time, she would soon move onto the next job site anyway, and the IRS would lose track of her again for a period of time. If it is Karen's goal to eventually file bankruptcy and dismiss the large tax liability she has incurred, she could continue this "bob and weave" for the three years it takes for the bankruptcy statute to take effect (whereby her tax liability could be discharged in Chapter 7).

Levying Bank Accounts

It is important to say something here about funds kept in a banking institution. The IRS is able to "sweep" all funds from your bank or securities accounts and transfer them directly to the IRS for payment of taxes owed. You could possibly switch banks, but if the IRS finds out you have dollars there, they will simply sweep that account as well. A remedy for this is to open an account with a good friend or relative (parent, sibling). Your name should not be listed on the account nor your social security number, but you can be given check-writing privileges on someone else's account. Therefore, the social security number on the account will be your partner's and not yours. It is not illegal to open an account under someone else's name and social security number and still have check-writing privileges, and it will prevent the IRS from grabbing your money.

Single/Unemployed - Married/Both Unemployed
Large Tax Liability

It is actually a good time to file past tax returns when you are unemployed. This is because you will be basically uncollectible. If you file returns and able to show that you are currently unable to pay anything towards that current liability (providing you've been able to protect your assets via friendly liens or other asset-protecting maneuvers) the IRS will probably place a stay on your account. In other words, they would not ask you for any money until you become employed again. This is an excellent way to set up a zero payment plan. The IRS would postpone any collection activity and review your account at a later date. This could buy you a year to a year and a half before the IRS will look at your case again.

Single/Self-Employed

Mark is a self employed carpenter who hasn't filed his income tax returns in six years. He owes $35,000 to the IRS, including interest and penalties. Mark plans on paying his tax liability.

As soon as he files his tax returns, the IRS will place liens on all of his assets including his business equipment, even though he will enter into a payment agreement with them. In order to avoid this, Mark should do the following: Just after filing his returns, he should incorporate his business, thereby making it a separate, legal entity. Mark will still have to enter into a payment arrangement with the IRS, but it will prevent them from placing liens on his assets, including the business equipment, allowing him to continue operating his business unencumbered by liens.

Married/One Employed, One Self-Employed

In this scenario, we will discuss the same couple, but the first example will concern filing their tax returns married/jointly, the second example ,married/separately.

Married Filing Jointly

Bob and Jill are married with three children. Bob is self-employed, earning about $60,000 a year. Jill is employed by a law firm as a paralegal earning $40,000 per year. Bob has always taken care of their financial affairs and (to Jill's chagrin) has not filed their income tax returns for the last five years.

Bob and Jill's assets and liabilities are as follows:

Assets

Cash	$ 5,000
Stocks	10,000
401K (Jill's)	15,000
Personal Residence	180,000
Furnishings	25,000
Automobiles	20,000
	$255,000

Liabilities

Credit Cards	$ 12,000
Mortgage (personal residence)	100,000
Auto Loans	10,000
	($122,000)
Net Worth	$133,000

Tax-wise, Jill is in pretty good shape because she has withholding on her wages. Bob, however, is another story. Being self-employed with an average income of $60,000 without paying income taxes or self-employment tax for five years has created an enormous tax liability.

Let's examine what will happen if Bob and Jill file their returns married/jointly. First of all, they will owe approximately $150,000 in tax, interest and penalties. The IRS collection division will immediately place liens on all their assets.

Realistically, it will be extremely difficult, if not impossible, for Bob and Jill to enter into a payment agreement that will satisfy the IRS. Remember that they must pay their current taxes as well, plus make large monthly payments on the past due liability balance. Also, keep in mind that the IRS has 10 years to collect under the statute of limitations.

In a situation like this, it would be likely the IRS (in order to enter into an agreement) would "request" the $5,000 in cash, $10,000 in securities, and the $15,000 from the 401K. After this initial chunk of $30,000, Bob and Jill still owe $120,000. In a best case situation, the payments would be $2,376 per month, assuming a 7% federal interest rate amortized over 5 years.

Obviously, this would place extreme pressure on the couple's cash flow. Their future financial life would be, at best, miserable. Being self-employed, Bob typically experiences extreme financial ups and downs which would hamper any type of payment agreement they may enter into with the IRS. If they *were* unable to keep the payment arrangement, the IRS would first levy Jill's wages and then auction off the home.

Assuming the IRS auction grosses $150,000 on the home, Bob and Jill would first pay off the $100,000 mortgage to the bank. The remaining $50,000 would go towards their IRS debt, leaving them a balance of $70,000, not to mention the interest and penalties that will continue to mount.

After the auction, *if* Bob and Jill were able to enter into a new payment agreement *and* the IRS would agree to release the levy on Jill's wages, the IRS would still be looking to receive approximately $1,386 per month. ($70,000 over 5 years at 7%). Again, this time period would be generous. The IRS, of course, usually likes to get their money in a shorter time period.

Time to make an offer in compromise? (See Chapter 7.) Forget it. The IRS views situations like this as fully collectable. It is easy to see that this family has truly entered into financial hell. It's obvious in this case that married filing jointly may not be the best way to go.

Married Filing Separately

Let's assume now that Bob and Jill decide to file married/separately. First of all, Jill will probably be entitled to a slight refund because she has had income taxes withheld from her wages. Bob, however, will owe approximately $175,000 (remember, married filing separately creates a higher tax liability).

Before the returns are filed, we should:
Step #1
Separate liquid assets. Close out the bank and securities accounts and open new accounts in Jill's name only.

Step #2

File the returns.

The important thing to note here is that the IRS cannot go after *jointly held real assets.* The IRS can go after jointly held bank accounts or securities, but not real property. The reason to file separately in this type of situation is to protect joint assets. The IRS will place a lien on the home (in the amount of Bob's tax liability), but they will not be able to auction off the property because of the jointly-held nature of the asset.

Caution: If Jill dies, leaving her assets to Bob, that money is going to disappear quickly, right into the pockets of the IRS. Jill will need to have a will drawn up where she leaves her assets to someone other than her husband, or sets up a trust so that the IRS cannot touch it.

Reorganization of Ownership

Let's look at this same situation in another light. Bob could incorporate his business with Jill purchasing 100 percent of the stock. In this type of situation, Bob could continue to operate the business with Jill paying him a salary. My staff and I feel that this strategy is legal and justified, as long as Bob is being paid a reasonable or fair wage, i.e. comparable to others in that industry (although probably on the lower end of the scale).

If Bob and Jill reposition in this manner, The IRS can not pursue Jill because she is current with her taxes, so the business would be safe, as well as the couple's home because of its jointly-held nature. Also, the IRS' levy position is very weak because Bob is not being paid a lot of money. If the IRS *does* decide to levy Bob's wages, the amount would be insignificant. This would be a good time for Bob to make an offer in compromise (see Chapter 7), or Bob could file bankruptcy three years after the tax assessment date thereby, discharging the entire tax liability (see Chapter 8.)

If this strategy does come under the scrutiny of the IRS, you or your tax professional may want to point out that in many cases it is the wife who is financially responsible. For example, in this case the incorporation of Bob's business with Jill owning the stock is quite justified because she was the only person in this scenario who was financially competent. It would be important to point out that Jill was a skilled and talented financial administrator.

Married/Self-Employed in Same Business

In both of these instances, it is imperative to keep one of the spouses free from the tax liability. This is very important because it will help to protect assets and will give them the future maneuverability that they wouldn't have if both of them were tied-up with the tax liability.

Let's take, for example, a married couple that owns and operates a convenience store. Prior to filing the tax returns, one of the partners should be established as the owner of the business and the other as less active. Then the couple can file their returns married/separately. This will result in a higher tax liability, but the other spouse will be free from the burden of the taxes. This "tax-free" spouse can safely manage bank and securities accounts without fear of IRS levy.

Married Both Partners Employed

The "Friendly Lien"

Let's look at another situation. Chris and Donna are married with two children. They both work, but both of them are seriously underwithheld and have not filed tax returns for five years. Separating the income and filing separately will not work - we just come up with an even larger tax liability. In this circumstance it simply boils down to filing the joint return and trying to settle with the IRS. How do we protect assets?

With interest and penalties, Chris and Donna owe the IRS a total of $75,000 which, in their estimation, they will never be able to pay. In fact, it looks as though they are heading toward some type of bankruptcy procedure. Their only real asset is their home, worth about $100,000, and they still have an outstanding mortgage of $75,000. We know that after we file the returns, the IRS will place a lien on the home thereby taking the equity in it. Plus, there's the possibility that if Chris and Donna default on their payment arrangement the IRS can actually auction off the house. Remember, Chris and Donna have two children. They know they owe the IRS the money, but they need to provide shelter for their family. What can they do?

Let's also assume that over the years, Donna's parents loaned the couple about $40,000. If Donna's parents put her through college, she may wish to pay them back. If Donna were to acknowledge this debt she could suggest that her parents place a "friendly" lien on their house for the $40,000 owed them.

(Think about it. Who would you rather owe? The IRS or your parents?) This friendly lien should be filed *prior* to filing the returns. When the returns are filed, the IRS will place their own lien on the home, but they will be in a third position to the other two mortgage holders (first the bank, then Donna's parents), rendering the IRS lien ineffective.

The friendly lien is a useful effective tool in dealing with the IRS. There is one important point, however. The debt involved must be genuine. Promissory notes need to be executed and the lien must be filed with the county.

The Actual Tax Forms

If you have not filed for several years, you will probably have trouble finding tax forms for those years. When filing your past tax returns, you cannot use the current year's forms and fill in dated information. You will need to use the appropriate tax forms for those particular years involved. Also, if you have moved around from state to state, this also presents problems. You will need to locate tax forms for each state involved and for the specific years owed. Often, even the IRS doesn't have these forms available and they can be hard to get. This is one of the advantages of *Tax Research Service, Inc.*, a library reference and tax advice company I began in 1990. We carry federal forms dating back to the late seventies, and state forms for all fifty states (see Chapter 9).

Final Word

When filing your tax returns it is important that you file all of the past-due returns at the same time so that you have the same tax assessment date for all years involved. This will greatly simplify measures when it comes to counting down the statute of limitations, especially if you should decide to file for bankruptcy once the three year bankruptcy statute has been met.

Also, prior to filing, I recommend my clients make needed purchases, such as a new vehicle - especially when there are several years of delinquent returns resulting in a large tax liability. After you file the tax returns, you will not be able to make any substantial purchases because a) your credit will be damaged, and b) the IRS will take all of your available cash. If you make needed purchases on credit prior to filing your past tax returns, you will also have the payments for these items listed on your income and expense analysis, which will help to scale down a monthly payment arrangement with the IRS. In collection cases where bankruptcy is not a possibility (at least until three years have passed from the tax assessment date) you will need to position yourself as well as possible prior to the filing of the tax returns.

Remember, your overall plan needs to be in place before you file your income tax returns. It is key to protecting your interests, assets, and overall lifestyle. Have a strategy *before* you file.

TWO

Postfiling Section

"The Chancellor of the Exchequer is a man whose duties make him more or less of a taxing machine. He is intrusted with a certain amount of misery which it is his duty to distribute as fairly as he can."
  - *Robert Lowe, Viscount Sherbrooke*
     House of Commons, 11 April 1870

6

Dealing With Collections

Who are IRS collection agents and were they trained by the KGB? Do they care if you are left on the streets, penniless? Are they really warm human beings after work hours?

Perhaps you have your own ideas on this subject. What we do know is that they are one tough group to deal with. Let's face it, most of the laws favor them and their ability to collect past due taxes. This chapter addresses strategies for helping you survive IRS collection tactics.

After the filing of the tax returns, you will be dealing directly with the collection division. There are three things that you can do in the meantime that will help you prepare for collection:

1. You will need to complete a Collection Information Statement, Form 433A (individual) and/or 433B (business).
2. You will need to complete an Installment Agreement Request, Form 9465.
3. It may be necessary to meet with an IRS collection agent if the liability is in excess of $10,000.

(These forms can be obtained from you local IRS office.)

Collection

Collection Information Statement (Form 433A/B)

In many nonfiler situations there are large tax liabilities involved. In order for the IRS to determine a payment arrangement, they will require you (or your tax practitioner) to fill out a Collection Information Statement, which is Form 433A, and for businesses, Form 433B (see illustrations). If you own your own business or are self-employed, you will need to fill out both forms.

These forms are rather simple. They are comparable to filling out a credit application for a bank, listing assets and liabilities, income and expenses. *It is extremely important that these forms be completed accurately under penalty of perjury. Also, your payment arrangement will be determined by these statements and you will be living within these guidelines for possibly the next ten years.* (Another reason for making sure that all of the applicable strategies are in place before filing the returns and filling out the collection information statement.)

Regarding the income and expense analysis on the fourth page of form 433A, the IRS will take the net income and subtract the expenses listed. They will expect to be paid the difference. IRS agents are *notorious* for wanting to trim down the expense side of the ledger, leaving you with very little to live on. For example, if you have a net monthly income of $5,000 and expenses of $3,500, the IRS would want the difference of $1,500. The problem with this is that seldom does life ever work out to exact expenses. You must try to allow enough room for unexpected or miscellaneous items, such as unusual medical expenses, care for elderly parents, care for children, and unusual maintenance bills.

Once you enter into a payment agreement with the IRS it is difficult to modify it. There's nothing worse than agreeing to a payment schedule only to find that, three or four months down the road, the terms are unacceptable. Don't wait to argue these figures until *after* you've made the agreement. Argue heartily before you agree to any terms.

When computing income, *don't include overtime or bonuses and go low on commissions* if this happens to be your source of income. In all cases, only include income you are guaranteed of receiving.

When computing expenses, figure them as high as possible. For example, let's assume you are driving a three year old car and payments are $400 per month for another 12 months. One of the favorite tools used by revenue officers is to schedule payment increases as your liabilities are paid off. The agent handling your case will want to increase the monthly IRS payment by $400 when the auto is paid off. However, it has been my experience that it will cost an individual about the same amount per month to keep the car on the road due to maintenance. Be insistent with the agent. It is ludicrous to think that you will be driving a vehicle that's 4, 5, 6 years old or more and won't have high monthly maintenance bills.

Regarding the asset section of the balance sheet, you will want to use conservative values on all assets. By conservative I mean "forced sale" values. Assume that your assets are being auctioned off and use values that you would (might) get for them. When computing your asset values, do not use a best case scenario. Always assume the worst. Use values you might expect to receive if these items were sold very quickly.

Regarding liabilities, include every single one you can think of - even liabilities that you might never be able, or don't intend, to pay. For example, let's assume you owe a hospital $10,000. You may never be able to pay them. You may plan on filing bankruptcy at some time in the future and this debt will be discharged. Nevertheless, this debt is still a verifiable liability and it should be listed as such on the balance sheet. After all, if you had the money, you would pay the debt to the hospital.

Let's also assume that you would like to pay back the hospital in monthly payments of $500. Even though, in reality, you cannot afford to pay this debt, a payment should be listed as a monthly expense because it is a bona fide, justifiable debt.

The same thing is true of certain personal loans you may have received from family or friends, but have not, or possibly will not, ever re-pay. As long as the debts are bona fide debts, list them. Just because you cannot afford to re-pay certain debts does not mean that the IRS should be able to "shut out" certain liabilities. After all, the IRS is not going to dismiss the liability owed to them simply because you cannot afford to pay it. As long as you have bona fide, verifiable debts, include them on the liability side of the balance sheet.

See Chapter Seven for more information on the 433A regarding filing an Offer in Compromise.

Form 433-A
(Rev. October 1992)

Department of the Treasury — Internal Revenue Service

Collection Information Statement for Individuals

NOTE: Complete all blocks, except shaded areas. Write "N/A" (not applicable) in those blocks that do not apply.

1. Taxpayer(s) name(s) and address	2. Home phone number ( )	3. Marital status
County _____	4.a. Taxpayer's social security number	b. Spouse's social security number

Section I. — Employment Information

5. Taxpayer's employer or business (name and address)	a. How long employed	b. Business phone number ( )	c. Occupation
	d. Number of exemptions claimed on Form W-4	e. Paydays	f. (Check appropriate box) ☐ Wage earner ☐ Partner ☐ Sole proprietor

6. Spouse's employer or business (name and address)	a. How long employed	b. Business phone number ( )	c. Occupation
	d. Number of exemptions claimed on Form W-4	e. Paydays	f. (Check appropriate box) ☐ Wage earner ☐ Partner ☐ Sole proprietor

Section II. — Personal Information

7. Name, address and telephone number of next of kin or other reference	8. Other names or aliases	9. Previous address(es)

10. Age and relationship of dependents living in your household (exclude yourself and spouse)

11. Date of Birth	a. Taxpayer	b. Spouse	12. Latest filed income tax return (tax year)	a. Number of exemptions claimed	b. Adjusted Gross Income

Section III. — General Financial Information

13. Bank accounts (Include Savings & Loans, Credit Unions, IRA and Retirement Plans, Certificates of Deposit, etc.)

Name of Institution	Address	Type of Account	Account No.	Balance
			Total (Enter in Item 21)	

Form **433-A** (Rev. 10-92)

433-A.1

110 • FAILURE TO FILE

Section III - *continued*   General Financial Information

14. Bank charge cards, Credit Unions, Savings and Loans, Lines of credit

Type of Account or Card	Name and Address of Financial Institution	Monthly Payment	Credit Limit	Amount Owed	Credit Available
	Totals *(Enter in Item 27)* ▶				

15. Safe deposit boxes rented or accessed *(List all locations, box numbers, and contents.)*

16.	Real Property *(Brief description and type of ownership)*	Physical Address
a.		
		County _____
b.		
		County _____
c.		
		County _____

17.	Life Insurance *(Name of Company)*	Policy Number	Type	Face Amount	Available Loan Value
			Total *(Enter in Item 23)* ▶		

18. Securities *(stocks, bonds, mutual funds, money market funds, government securities, etc.)*:

Kind	Quantity or Denomination	Current Value	Where Located	Owner of Record

19. Other information relating to your financial condition. If you check the yes box, please give dates and explain on page 4, Additional Information or Comments:

a. Court proceedings	☐ Yes ☐ No	b. Bankruptcies	☐ Yes ☐ No
c. Repossessions	☐ Yes ☐ No	d. Recent transfer of assets for less than full value	☐ Yes ☐ No
e. Anticipated increase in income	☐ Yes ☐ No	f. Participant or beneficiary to trust, estate, profit sharing, etc.	☐ Yes ☐ No

Form **433-A**   page 2   (Rev. 10-92)

433-A.2   Published by Tax Management Inc., a Subsidiary of The Bureau of National Affairs, Inc.   12/14/92

Section IV.   Asset and Liability Analysis

Description	Current Market Value	Liabilities Balance Due	Equity in Asset	Amount of Monthly Payment	Name and Address of Lien/Note Holder/Obligee	Date Pledged	Date of Final Payment
20. Cash							
21. Bank accounts *(from Item 13)*							
22. Securities *(from Item 18)*							
23. Cash or loan value of Insur.							
24. Vehicles *(Model, year, license, tag #)*							
a.							
b.							
c.							
25. Real property *(From Section III, Item 16)* a.							
b.							
c.							
26. Other assets							
a.							
b.							
c.							
d.							
e.							
27. Bank revolving credit *(from Item 14)*							
28. Other Liabilities *(Including judgments, notes, and other charge accounts)* a.							
b.							
c.							
d.							
e.							
f.							
g.							
29. Federal taxes owed							
30. Totals				$	$		

Internal Revenue Service Use Only Below This Line

Financial Verification/Analysis

Item	Date Information or Encumbrance Verified	Date Property Inspected	Estimated Forced Sale Equity
Personal Residence			
Other Real Property			
Vehicles			
Other Personal Property			
State Employment *(Husband and Wife)*			
Income Tax Return			
Wage Statements *(Husband and Wife)*			
Sources of Income/Credit *(D&B Report)*			
Expenses			
Other Assets/Liabilities			

Form **433-A**   page 3   (Rev. 10-92)

112 • FAILURE TO FILE

Section V. Monthly Income and Expense Analysis

Income			Necessary Living Expenses	
Source	Gross	Net		
31. Wages/Salaries *(Taxpayer)*	$	$	42. Rent *(Do not show mortgage listed in item 25)*	$
32. Wages/Salaries *(Spouse)*			43. Groceries (no. of people _____)	
33. Interest - Dividends			44. Allowable installment payments *(IRS use only)*	
34. Net business income *(from Form 433-B)*			45. Utilities (Gas $ _____ Water $ _____	
35. Rental income			Electric $ _____ Phone $ _____)	
36. Pension *(Taxpayer)*			46. Transportation	
37. Pension *(Spouse)*			47. Insurance (Life $ _____ Health $ _____	
38. Child Support			Home $ _____ Car $ _____)	
39. Alimony			48. Medical *(Expenses not covered in item 47)*	
40. Other			49. Estimated tax payments	
			50. Court ordered payments	
			51. Other expenses *(specify)*	
41. Total Income	$	$	52. Total Expenses *(IRS use only)*	
			53. Net difference *(income less necessary living expenses)* *(IRS use only)*	$

Certification Under penalties of perjury, I declare that to the best of my knowledge and belief this statement of assets, liabilities, and other information is true, correct, and complete.

54. Your signature	55. Spouse's signature *(if joint return was filed)*	56. Date

Additional information or comments:

Internal Revenue Service Use Only Below This Line

Explain any difference between Item 53 and the installment agreement payment amount:

Name of originator and IDRS assignment number:	Date

Form **433-A** page 4 (Rev. 10-92)   ✶U.S.GPO 1992-0-343-049/71911

433-A.4   Published by Tax Management Inc., a Subsidiary of The Bureau of National Affairs, Inc.   12/14/92

Dealing With Collections • 113

Form **433-B**
(Rev. June 1991)

Department of the Treasury — Internal Revenue Service

Collection Information Statement for Businesses

(If you need additional space, please attach a separate sheet)

NOTE: Complete all blocks, except shaded areas. Write "N/A" *(not applicable)* in those blocks that do not apply.

1. Name and address of business	2. Business phone number ( )
	3. (Check appropriate box) ☐ Sole proprietor ☐ Other *(specify)* ☐ Partnership ☐ Corporation
County____	
4. Name and title of person being interviewed	5. Employer Identification Number 6. Type of business

7. Information about owner, partners, officers, major shareholder, etc.

Name and Title	Effective Date	Home Address	Phone Number	Social Security Number	Total Shares or Interest

Section I.   General Financial Information

8. Latest filed income tax return ▶	Form	Tax Year ended	Net income before taxes

9. Bank accounts *(List all types of accounts including payroll and general, savings, certificates of deposit, etc.)*

Name of Institution	Address	Type of Account	Account Number	Balance
		Total *(Enter in Item 17)* ▶		

10. Bank credit available *(Lines of credit, etc.)*

Name of Institution	Address	Credit Limit	Amount Owed	Credit Available	Monthly Payments
Totals *(Enter in Items 24 or 25 as appropriate)*		▶			

11. Location, box number, and contents of all safe deposit boxes rented or accessed

Form 433-B (Rev. 6-91)

114 • FAILURE TO FILE

Section I - *continued*   **General Financial Information**

12. Real property

	Brief Description and Type of Ownership	Physical Address
a.		County _____
b.		County _____
c.		County _____
d.		County _____

13. Life insurance policies owned with business as beneficiary

Name Insured	Company	Policy Number	Type	Face Amount	Available Loan Value
		Total *(Enter in Item 19)*		▶	

14a. Additional information regarding financial condition *(Court proceedings, bankruptcies filed or anticipated, transfers of assets for less than full value, changes in market conditions, etc.; include information regarding company participation in trusts, estates, profit-sharing plans, etc.)*

b. If you know of any person or organization that borrowed or otherwise provided funds to pay net payrolls:	a. Who borrowed funds?
	b. Who supplied funds?

15. Accounts/Notes receivable *(Include current contract jobs, loans to stockholders, officers, partners, etc.)*

Name	Address	Amount Due	Date Due	Status
		$		
	Total *(Enter in Item 18)* ▶	$		

Form 433-B (Rev. 6-91)

Section II.   Asset and Liability Analysis

Description (a)	Cur. Mkt. Value (b)	Liabilities Bal. Due (c)	Equity in Asset (d)	Amt. of Mo. Pymt. (e)	Name and Address of Lien/Note Holder/Obligee (f)	Date Pledged (g)	Date of Final Pymt. (h)
16. Cash on hand							
17. Bank accounts							
18. Accounts/Notes receivable							
19. Life insurance loan value							
20. Real property (from Item 12) a.							
b.							
c.							
d.							
21. Vehicles (Model, year, and license) a.							
b.							
c.							
22. Machinery and equipment (Specify) a.							
b.							
c.							
23. Merchandise inventory (Specify) a.							
b.							
24. Other assets (Specify) a.							
b.							
25. Other liabilities (Including notes and judgments) a.							
b.							
c.							
d.							
e.							
f.							
g.							
h.							
26. Federal taxes owed							
27. Total							

Form 433-B (Rev. 6-91)

11/4/91   Published by Tax Management Inc., a Subsidiary of The Bureau of National Affairs, Inc.   433-B.3

116 • Failure To File

Section III.   Income and Expense Analysis

The following information applies to income and expenses during the period _____ to _____

Accounting method used

Income			Expenses	
28. Gross receipts from sales, services, etc.	$	34. Materials purchased		$
29. Gross rental income		35. Net wages and salaries Number of Employees _____		
30. Interest		36. Rent		
31. Dividends		37. Allowable installment payments *(IRS use only)*		
32. Other income *(Specify)*		38. Supplies		
		39. Utilities/Telephone		
		40. Gasoline/Oil		
		41. Repairs and maintenance		
		42. Insurance		
		43. Current taxes		
		44. Other *(Specify)*		
33. Total Income ▶	$	45. Total Expenses *(IRS use only)* ▶		$
		46. Net difference *(IRS use only)* ▶		

Certification   Under penalties of perjury, I declare that to the best of my knowledge and belief this statement of assets, liabilities, and other information is true, correct, and complete.

47. Signature

48. Date

Internal Revenue Service Use Only Below This Line

Financial Verification/Analysis

Item	Date Information or Encumbrance Verified	Date Property Inspected	Estimated Forced Sale Equity
Sources of Income/Credit (D&B Report)			
Expenses			
Real Property			
Vehicles			
Machinery and Equipment			
Merchandise			
Accounts/Notes Receivable			
Corporate Information, if Applicable			
U.C.C. : Senior/Junior Lienholder			
Other Assets/Liabilities:			

Explain any difference between Item 46 (or P&L) and the installment agreement payment amount:

Name of Originator and IDRS assignment number

Date

Page 4   Form 433-B (Rev. 6-91)

Installment Agreement Request (Form 9465)

If you have chosen not to use a tax practitioner, it is certainly important at this point to contact the IRS prior to a revenue officer contacting you. Normally, you will have 4 to 8 weeks after the filing of the returns before being contacted by the IRS. Therefore, I recommend that after about 4 weeks from filing (if not sooner) you sit down and figure out what you'd like your proposed payment arrangement to be, using the information you filled out on the 433A/B.

If you are using a tax professional, you can meet with them at this time to discuss your payment arrangement. They should then submit a Power of Attorney/Form 2848 (signed by you), the Collection Information Statement(s) and the Installment Agreement Request/Form 9465 (see illustration).

Using a tax professional will benefit you during the collection period because you won't have to meet with somewhat probing revenue officers and your tax professional will act as a buffer between you and the collection division.

You can send the 433A/B in attached to your tax returns or, in order to buy more time before having to make payments, you can wait 4 to 6 weeks after the filing of the returns and send the 433A/B and the Installment Agreement Request together. Whichever method you choose, it is best to contact the IRS prior to them contacting you, and to try and enter into a payment agreement prior to adverse levy or lien activity. *Remember, the income and expense analysis on the 433-A (or B) is critical in entering into a successful agreement with the IRS.* If there are any circumstances that require explanations, be sure to include them in the space provided or add additional

118 • FAILURE TO FILE

| Form **9465**
(Rev. December 1992) | Department of the Treasury – Internal Revenue Service
Installment Agreement Request | OMB Clearance No.
1545-1350
Expires 12/31/93 |

General Information

If you can't pay the amount you owe in full at this time, please request an installment agreement by completing this form. Specify the amount of the monthly payment you propose to make in the block marked "Proposed monthly payment amount."

We encourage you to make your payments as large as possible to lower penalty and interest charges. Under law, these charges continue to increase until you pay the balance in full.

Please attach this form to the front of your tax return or to the notice we sent you, and mail it to the appropriate IRS office.

Make your check or money order payable to the Internal Revenue Service, and mark the payment with your name, address, taxpayer identification number, form number and tax period. If you have any questions about this procedure, please call our toll-free number **1-800-829-1040**.

Within 30 days, we will let you know if your request for an installment agreement is approved or denied, or if we need more information.

Taxpayer name(s) as shown on the tax return			Taxpayer identification number *(SSN for primary & secondary filers)* or EIN
Address		City	State	ZIP Code
Business telephone number *(include area code and extension number, if any)*	Most convenient time for us to call you	Home telephone number *(include area code)*	Most convenient time for us to call you
Form number and tax period	Amount paid with return	Amount owed on return	Proposed monthly payment amount
			Amount I am able to pay each month	Date each month I am able to make the payment *(Must be the 1st through the 28th day)*
Your signature			Date
Spouse's signature *(joint returns only)*			Date

Privacy Act and Paperwork Reduction Act Notice

We ask for the information on this form under authority of Internal Revenue Code sections 6001, 6011, 6012(a), 6109, and 6159 and their regulations. We use this information to process your request for an installment agreement. The principal reason we need your name and social security number is to secure proper identification. We require this information to gain access to the tax information in our files and properly respond to your request. If you do not disclose the information, the IRS may not be able to process your request.

The time needed to complete and file this form will vary depending on individual circumstances. The estimated average time is 10 minutes.

If you have comments concerning the accuracy of this time estimate or suggestions for making this form more simple, we would be happy to hear from you. You can write to both the **Internal Revenue Service**, Washington, DC 20224, Attention: IRS Reports Clearance Officer, T:FP, and the **Office of Management and Budget Paperwork Reduction Project (1545-1350)**, Washington, DC 20503. **DO NOT** send this form to either of these offices. Instead, refer to the instructions above.

*U.S. GPO: 1993-343-049/71975   Catalog No. 14842Y   Form **9465** (Rev. 12/92)

information sheets. Also, if the agreement is not accepted, be prepared to send additional documentation to support your position. In most cases agreements can be reached in this manner.

Important

After filing the returns, the collection people will be directly involved so we do know that a levy is probably imminent. It is important to try and enter into a payment agreement prior to a levy. To be on the safe side, though, it's a good idea to keep very little money in your bank accounts and be ready to respond very quickly to the IRS in the event of a wage levy. By all means, contact the IRS before they contact you.

Meeting with a Collections Officer

It is always best to try and get a payment agreement going with the Form 9465. If your tax liability is over $10,000 there will be an agent assigned to your case, but if you can enter into an agreement with the Form 9465, you may not need to meet with an IRS agent. Sometimes, however, the IRS prefers to have an agent sit down with you and review the 433A/B and your Installment Agreement Request.

It is very tough to handle a collection case by yourself. It will be easier if you can keep from being intimidated by the collection people and not necessarily agree with everything they say in terms of collecting your money. If you disagree with them for any reason or feel that you are not being treated fairly, you can ask to speak with the collection agent's supervisor.

Things you should not do when meeting with an IRS Revenue Officer *(a nice euphemism for collection agent)*:

1. Never volunteer any information regarding retirement plans. (The IRS cannot force you to withdraw funds from a retirement plan. They can suggest this be done, but they have no right to force you to use these funds to pay off a tax liability.)
2. Never volunteer any information about your ability or the possibility of borrowing money, whether that be from banks, credit cards, family, or friends. The IRS cannot force you to take out a loan in order to pay off a tax liability, even if you have credit available (bank, credit cards).
3. If the revenue officer pressures you on either of the above two issues, respond by saying that you're "not sure", you "don't know", you "will have to look into the matter". Do not commit in any way regarding either point. If you state that you will look into the matter, don't even commit to when you'll get back to them. Simply state that you'll get back to them "at a later time" or when you "have an answer to the question".
4. Lastly, do not sign anything at the meeting. If the agent prepares forms for you to sign, particularly any type of payment agreement forms, do not sign them. Tell the agent that you wish to take the forms/papers home and

review them. As I've stated previously, IRS agents are particularly skilled at intimidation techniques and sometimes they will try to pressure an individual into signing an agreement that they haven't had the opportunity of reviewing. Just being in an IRS office is intimidating and you will probably want to get out of the meeting as quickly as possible, but do not let yourself be bullied into anything, particularly signing a payment agreement.

Things you *should* do when meeting with an IRS Revenue Officer:

1. If your credit is poor, you should take a copy of your TRW (credit report) with you to the meeting because it could help to prove your case, i.e. that you are not in the best financial position to take on a large payment plan; that you need generous terms.
2. Also, take any documentation of any outstanding liabilities in order to prove to the agent that they actually exist, and any documentation of income and particularly expenses, as listed on the Form 433A.

Automated Collections

Several years ago the IRS set up an operation known as the Automated Collection Service (ACS). The ACS is a computer-based on-line inventory of delinquent tax accounts and delinquent tax investigations for tax liabilities under $10,000. ACS call sites are responsible for the resolution and collection of delinquent accounts and for securing delinquent returns through concentrated telephone contacts. ACS also causes the filing of notices of tax lien and the service of notices of levy.

The phone number to contact the ACS call site nearest you can be obtained by calling 1-800-829-1040.

One of the difficult aspects of dealing with automated collections is getting through to them in the first place. Their phone lines seem to be busy non-stop throughout the day, making it extremely difficult just to have a conversation. This being the case, you must bear down and be persistent. One of the techniques used in my office is to automatically dial the number, because it sometimes takes dozens of attempts before ever connecting. Also, if you have a speaker phone, you will be able to stay on hold for an endless amount of time until you get a response.

Another problem in dealing with ACS is that if you are missing certain pieces of information and need to get back to people. It is often very difficult to get the same person because the system is designed for service at random. The collection agents do make notes on the computer screen and the notes are available for subsequent agents, but you may need to re-negotiate. Make sure you have all of the information they will need; the 433A/B filled out completely, tax returns, notices, and any answers to questions regarding wages and withholding, like paycheck stubs.

To avoid having to re-negotiate with a new collection agent, you may try faxing the information to the agent you originally dealt with, requesting a call-back. This is a particularly good strategy to employ when you don't want to build a rapport with a brand new agent.

Buying Time

In dealing with cases where the tax liability is over $10,000 a collection agent will be assigned to the case. Buying time is critical in these situations. For one thing, you may not be able to pay anything to the IRS right away. Secondly, you may be marching towards a Chapter 7 bankruptcy, which can occur 3 years from the assessment date of the tax (see Chapter 8). If this is the case, every month that goes by without making a payment is a payment you will never have to make.

There are several ways to buy time, and this is a lot easier done when you are using a tax professional. For example, let's assume your case will be assigned to a revenue officer once you file the returns. When the revenue officer contacts you, you would be able to refer them to your tax practitioner, to whom you've given power of attorney. By taking his or her time in getting information to and from the IRS, your tax practitioner could burn up 2 or 3 weeks.

Another advantage to using a tax practitioner is that it distances you from the IRS. Having to communicate via a neutral party (tax professional) can sometimes burn up three to six months of the statute period. Especially during the negotiation period, if your tax preparer insists on discussing *all* matters with you before ever moving forward, this delay tactic could buy an additional six months, possibly even a year. It's actually very easy to put off revenue officers. The IRS is understaffed and when you drag your feet a bit, it's easy for an agent to get involved in other cases. Remember, the average collection agent is assigned approximately 100 cases at any point in time. Important: If you are dealing with the IRS one on one, it is important that you always appear cordial and cooperative with the IRS. Taking your time is not the same as ignoring them.

The Bob and Weave

There is another interesting point regarding collection arrangements. If it is simply your goal to buy enough time to get to the point where you can file for bankruptcy, or if your goal is to end the statute of limitations, the IRS really won't know how to contact you if you change jobs. In other words, say in April 1993 you set up a payment arrangement with the IRS paying $500 per month. In August of 1993 you change jobs, simultaneously ceasing to make IRS payments. The IRS will file a levy against your previous employer, but it will be an ineffective levy because you are no longer employed there. The IRS won't be able to locate you until you file your income tax returns for the following year.

Caution: If you have opted for this tactic, make sure you don't answer the door. Screen all telephone calls and refuse any certified mail.

Failed Payment Arrangements

After setting up the payment arrangement, what happens if a payment is missed? The IRS immediately issues a "default" letter along with notice of intent to levy (see illustration). Prompt contact with the IRS must be made in order to avoid adverse collection *without further notification.*

The IRS can, without further notification, garnishee wages, file a levy against your bank account or seize other assets. If you have employed a tax practitioner, it is imperative that you notify him or her immediately if you fall off track with payments so they can contact the IRS and set up a new payment arrangement. I have had some clients who have fallen off their payment arrangements several times. The agents are usually very hard on them, but if you explain the circumstances and can come up with good reasons as to why you failed to keep the arrangement (tangible human reasons, not just that you had too many expenses) they usually work things out.

Once you get into collection, don't let things get out of hand. It is important to keep these collection deals alive or you may experience the iron grip of an IRS levy - or worse.

Case Study:

Phil and Susan had entered into a collection agreement with the IRS where they were paying $1,500 per month. Susan was a homemaker and Phil a self-employed commercial real estate agent. Phil's income would go from $50,000 in one month to zero for the next several months. This extreme fluctuation in income is what caused them to get into trouble in the first place.

Phil had defaulted on his collection arrangements on three previous occasions. When he entered into round four, the collection agent was extremely irate. However, I pointed out that rigid IRS procedures did not lend themselves well to this

126 • FAILURE TO FILE

```
COPY        RPT                                    ACR   003737
         417  3801                 CAF          5  17247-478-90164-3           9338
                           P 901 766 302
```

Department of the Treasury
Internal Revenue Service
CINCINNATI   OH   45999

```
                                      DATE OF NOTICE: 10-04-93      9344    CP523
                                      TAXPAYER IDENTIFYING NUMBER:
                                    FORM 1040           TAX PERIOD 12-31-89
```

FOR ASSISTANCE YOU MAY CALL US AT:

237-0800 LOCAL DETROIT
1-800-829-1040 OTHER MI

OR YOU MAY WRITE TO US AT THE ADDRESS SHOWN AT THE LEFT. IF YOU WRITE, BE SURE TO ATTACH THE BOTTOM PART OF THIS NOTICE.

DEFAULTED INSTALLMENT AGREEMENT - NOTICE OF INTENT TO LEVY

OUR RECORDS INDICATE YOU ARE NOT MEETING THE TERMS OF YOUR INSTALLMENT PLAN. OUR AGREEMENT WITH YOU STATES THAT WE MAY WITHDRAW YOUR INSTALLMENT PLAN AND COLLECT THE ENTIRE AMOUNT OF YOUR TAX LIABILITY IF YOU DO NOT MAKE YOUR PAYMENTS AS AGREED.

TO PREVENT THIS ACTION, YOU MUST, WITHIN 10 DAYS FROM THE DATE OF THIS NOTICE BRING YOUR PAYMENTS UP TO DATE.

MAKE YOUR CHECK OR MONEY ORDER PAYABLE TO THE INTERNAL REVENUE SERVICE. WRITE YOUR TAXPAYER IDENTIFYING NUMBER (SOCIAL SECURITY OR EMPLOYER IDENTIFICATION NUMBER) ON YOUR PAYMENT. THEN, SEND YOUR PAYMENT TO US IN THE ENCLOSED ENVELOPE WITH THE BOTTOM PART OF THIS NOTICE TO ASSURE PROMPT AND ACCURATE CREDIT.

IF WE HAVE NOT ALREADY DONE SO, WE MAY FILE A NOTICE OF FEDERAL TAX LIEN AT ANY TIME TO PROTECT THE GOVERNMENT'S INTEREST. THAT IS A PUBLIC NOTICE TO YOUR CREDITORS THAT THE GOVERNMENT HAS A RIGHT TO YOUR INTERESTS IN YOUR CURRENT PROPERTY, INCLUDING PROPERTY YOU ACQUIRE AFTER WE FILE THE LIEN.

IF YOU DO NOT COMPLY WITH THE TERMS OF THIS AGREEMENT WITHIN THE 10-DAY PERIOD, WE MAY, 30 DAYS FROM THE DATE OF THIS NOTICE, ISSUE A NOTICE OF LEVY WITHOUT FURTHER NOTICE TO YOU. THIS MEANS THE LAW ALLOWS US TO SEIZE YOUR PROPERTY OR RIGHTS TO PROPERTY SUCH AS ESTATE AND PERSONAL PROPERTY (FOR EXAMPLE, AUTOMOBILES AND BUSINESS ASSETS) TO COLLECT THE AMOUNT YOU STILL OWE. WE ALSO MAY LEVY (TAKE) YOUR WAGES, BANK ACCOUNTS, COMMISSIONS, AND OTHER INCOME. SEE THE ENCLOSED PUBLICATION FOR ADDITIONAL INFORMATION.

THE AMOUNT YOU OWE IS $15,719.60.

```
        WE FIGURED THIS AMOUNT BY ADDING:
            AMOUNT UNPAID FROM PRIOR NOTICES          $14,151.41
            ADDITIONAL LATE PAYMENT PENALTY              $702.39
            ADDITIONAL INTEREST                          $865.80
```

THE AMOUNT UNPAID FROM PRIOR NOTICES MAY INCLUDE TAX, PENALTIES, AND INTEREST YOU STILL OWE IRS. IT ALSO SHOULD REFLECT ANY CREDITS AND PAYMENTS WE RECEIVED SINCE THE LAST NOTICE WE SENT YOU.

IF YOU RECENTLY TOOK ACTION TO MEET THE ABOVE REQUEST OR IF YOU CANNOT PAY THE AMOUNT YOU OWE IN FULL, CONTACT OUR OFFICE IMMEDIATELY.

TO MAKE SURE IRS EMPLOYEES GIVE COURTEOUS RESPONSES AND CORRECT INFORMATION TO TAXPAYERS, A SECOND EMPLOYEE SOMETIMES LISTENS IN ON TELEPHONE CALLS.
KEEP THIS PART FOR YOUR RECORDS

RETURN THIS PART WITH YOUR PAYMENT OR INQUIRY

```
                                                        ACR
                              CAF                 5  17247-478-90164-3           9338
```

type of situation (inconsistent income) and flexibility was the order of the day. The agent finally agreed.

(See Chapter 8 for more on Chapter 13 bankruptcy for failed payment agreements.)

In this chapter we've discussed some tactics in dealing with the collection division. These tactics are generally designed to comply with a revenue officer's requests, but more importantly, to stall for time in order to delay payment arrangements. We also want to drag out this process in order to whittle away at the statute of limitations - but not to the detriment of the overall strategy.

"Neither will it be, that a people overlaid with taxes should ever become valiant and martial."
  - *Francis Bacon*

7

Offer In Compromise

SIMPLY SPEAKING, AN *offer in compromise is an attempt to settle a tax debt for a lesser amount than the actual liability.* This sounds simple enough, and some creditors may even be eager to accept an all-out cash settlement of a lesser amount, rather than taking payments for years. But remember, you're dealing with the IRS.

This entire book is primarily dedicated to the subject of income tax. However, it is important to note that an offer in compromise can be used for other types of tax as well; payroll taxes, estate taxes - any kind of tax that is owed qualifies for this program. Keep in mind, however, that *state income taxes will need to be dealt with on a local level.*

In the past, offers were not an effective bargaining tool with the Government because the IRS would rather wait out the statute of limitations in the hopes of collecting the past due taxes. However, the offer in compromise seems revitalized as a valid method for settling tax debts, probably to rake in some extra revenue.

When it comes to an offer in compromise, though, the IRS seems to seriously consider only large tax liabilities. Actually,

I have found them quite indifferent to compromising with those owing smaller tax liabilities (in the two to five thousand dollar range). Personally, I find this discriminatory, based on economic station. The *amount* of money owed is not supposed to be criteria for this program. Just because a person is in a lower income bracket doesn't mean they shouldn't be able to benefit from this program, if need be. Several times now I have mentioned this to IRS agents and they quickly do some backtracking. Being a government agency, the word "discrimination" doesn't exactly bode well with them, so this is an important tactic to keep in mind if you have a low tax liability and decide to file an offer in compromise.

As a rule, the IRS' policy is to accept an offer in compromise when:

(1) it is unlikely that the IRS can collect the tax liability in full; and

(2) the amount offered by the taxpayer reasonably reflects collection potential.

The IRS recognizes that an offer in compromise is a legitimate alternative to declaring a tax uncollectible. The IRS' goal in considering a taxpayer's offer in compromise is to achieve collection of what is potentially collectible at the earliest possible time and at the least cost to the government.

Compromise Objectives: The IRS' objectives in accepting an offer in compromise are:

* To resolve tax accounts which cannot be collected in full or the amount of which is legitimately disputed;
* To collect what can reasonably be collected at the earliest possible time and at the least cost to the government;
* To give taxpayers a fresh start toward future voluntary compliance with the tax laws; and

* To collect the taxes from funds or property beyond the reach of the IRS.

The offer form (Form 656) is fairly simple to fill out (see illustration). Just go through the form line by line. In addition, you will need to attach form 433A and/or 433B. The same rules for filling out this form apply as outline in Chapter Six. Also, the IRS agent will want to see evidence of current earnings, so attach a current pay stub if you are employed.

At this time you can include a check for the proposed offer amount. If the offer is rejected, your check will be returned to you, but I suggest waiting to submit the check until you know the offer is accepted.

Your offer can be mailed in or submitted to the IRS office nearest you.

The Offer Period

The offer period is that time between filing the offer in compromise until the time that the offer is either accepted or rejected. This is generally 4 to 6 months.

Advantage to the Offer in Compromise

One advantage to making an offer in compromise is that *all collection activity is suspended during the offer period.* This can be a great relief to the taxpayer, particularly if the IRS is doing things like levying wages, placing liens on assets, or

132 • FAILURE TO FILE

Form 656
(Rev. February 1992)

Department of the Treasury — Internal Revenue Service

Offer in Compromise

▶ File in Triplicate
▶ See Instructions Page 4

Name and Address of Taxpayers

For Official Use Only

Offer is (Check applicable box)
☐ Cash (Paid in full)
☐ Deferred payment

Serial Number

(Cashier's stamp)

Social Security Number

Employer Identification Number

To: Commissioner of Internal Revenue Service

Amount Paid
$

(1) This offer is being submitted by taxpayer-proponents to compromise a tax liability, plus statutory additions resulting from the failure to pay an Internal Revenue liability described as follows: _____
(Describe the specific tax liability, see instructions)

(2) The total sum of the offer is $ _____. If payment in full is not submitted with this offer, describe below when the payment will be made:

As required by section 6621 of the Internal Revenue Code, interest shall accrue on payments made from the date the offer is accepted and until the amount offered is paid in full. The interest will be compounded daily as required by Section 6622 of the Internal Revenue Code.

(3) All payments made with this offer are submitted voluntarily. The taxpayer-proponents request that the offer be accepted to compromise the tax liability described in paragraph (1). If the offer is rejected or withdrawn, the amount deposited will be refunded unless the taxpayer-proponents authorize in writing that the payment be applied to the liability. If an authorization is made, the date of payment will be considered the date the offer is rejected or withdrawn.

(4) In making this offer and as part of the consideration for the offer, the taxpayer-proponents agree: (a) to comply with all the provisions of the Internal Revenue Code relating to the filing of returns and the paying of taxes for a period of five (5) years following the acceptance of the offer; (b) that the United States shall retain all payments and credits made and applied to the tax liabilities being compromised, until the terms of the offer are satisfied; (c) that the United States shall be entitled to keep all amounts, including interest and penalties due to the taxpayer-proponents under the Internal Revenue laws because of any overpayment of any tax or other liability, for periods ending before the calendar year or extending through the calendar year in which the offer is accepted, and (d) to immediately return to the Internal Revenue Service any overpayment amount identified in (c) above, following the acceptance of the offer.

(5) The total amount that can be collected under the terms and conditions of this offer cannot exceed the amount of the tax liabilities being compromised plus statutory additions.

(6) It is also agreed that payments made under the terms of the offer shall be applied first to tax and penalty, in that order, due for the earliest tax period covered by this offer, then to tax and penalty for each succeeding tax period covered by this offer. No amount shall be applied to payment of interest until the tax and penalty liabilities for all tax periods covered by this offer have been paid.

(7) It is agreed that upon notice to the taxpayer-proponents that the offer has been accepted, the taxpayer-proponents shall have no right to contest in court or otherwise the amount of the liability to be compromised. In addition, if there is a default on any payment or any other condition required under the terms of the offer, the Commissioner of the Internal Revenue Service or delegated official, may (a) proceed immediately by suit to collect the entire unpaid balance of the offer; (b) proceed immediately by suit to collect as liquidated damages an amount equal to the liability sought to be compromised, minus any payments already received under the terms of the offer with interest on the unpaid balance accruing and applied as specified in paragraph (2), from the date of default; or (c) disregard the amount of the offer and apply all amounts previously paid under the offer against the amount of the liability compromised and, without further notice of any kind, assess and collect by levy or suit the balance of the liability. The right to appeal to the United States Tax Court and the statutory restrictions against assessment and collection are waived upon acceptance of this offer as stated in paragraph (8).

(8) The taxpayer-proponents agree to the waiver and suspension of any statutory periods of limitations for assessment and collection of the tax liability described in paragraph (1) while the offer is pending, during the time any amount offered remains unpaid and for one (1) year after the satisfaction of the terms of the offer. The offer shall be deemed pending from the date an authorized official of the Internal Revenue Service accepts taxpayer-proponents' waiver of the statutory periods of limitation and shall remain pending until an authorized official of the Internal Revenue Service formally, in writing, accepts, rejects or withdraws the offer. If there is an appeal with respect to this offer, the offer shall be deemed pending until the date the Appeals office formally accepts or rejects this offer in writing. If within thirty (30) days of being notified of a right to protest a determination with regard to this offer, no protest is filed, the taxpayer-proponents agree to waive the right to a hearing before the Appeals office for this offer in compromise.

(9) The following facts and reasons are submitted as grounds for acceptance of this offer: _____

(If space is insufficient, please attach a supporting statement)

(10) It is understood that this offer will be considered and acted upon in due course and that it does not relieve the taxpayers from the liability sought to be compromised unless and until the offer is accepted in writing by the Commissioner or a delegated official, and there has been full compliance with the terms of the offer.

I accept the waiver of statutory period of limitations for the Internal Revenue Service.		Under penalties of perjury, I declare that I have examined this offer, including accompanying schedules and statements, and to the best of my knowledge and belief, it is true, correct and complete.	
Signature of authorized Internal Revenue Service Official		Signature of Taxpayer-proponent	Date
Title	Date	Signature of Taxpayer-proponent	Date

Part 1 IRS Copy

Form **656** (Rev. 2-92)

5/4/92   Published by Tax Management Inc., a Subsidiary of The Bureau of National Affairs, Inc.   656.1

Offer in Compromise *continued*

For Office Use Only	
Liability Incurred By *(List taxpayers included under same account no.)*	Kind of Liability *(Complete description)*

Date Notice of Lien Filed	Place Notice of Lien Filed	Was Bond Filed? *(If yes, attach copy)* ☐ Yes ☐ No
Were Assets Pledged as Security? *(If yes, attach complete information)*	Periods Involved and Dates Returns Filed for Offers Involving Delinquency Penalties Only	Were Tax Collection Waivers Filed? *(If yes, attach copies)* ☐ Yes ☐ No

Attach Transcript of Accounts

threatening to auction off assets. On several occasions, my clients have opted to file an offer in compromise just to get wage levies released, providing themselves with a little financial relief. You may also want to consider this tactic.

However, to file an offer in compromise *all income tax returns must be filed.* So, if an offer is being used in order to get a wage levy released, you will need to prepare your income tax returns as quickly as possible and file them first.

Disadvantage to the Offer in Compromise

The disadvantage to filing an offer in compromise is that the statute of limitations is suspended *plus an additional six months is added,* thereby lengthening the collection period. Since the offer period can also take six months, this may mean adding a full year to the statute of limitations if the offer is rejected.

The Timing of the Offer

A critical part of the offer process is knowing *when* to file an offer in relationship to the statute of limitations. The bankruptcy statute must also be taken into consideration.

Take, for instance, the Chapter 7 bankruptcy (more in Chapter 8). Income taxes can be discharged under Chapter 7 bankruptcy after three years have passed from the tax assessment date. Of course, most people want to avoid bankruptcy if at all possible. However, if the offer in compromise fails you do not want to place yourself in a position of extending the statute of limitations, thereby forcing you to make installment payments for an additional period of time (the extra six months added to the statute). Strategically, it is best to wait to file an offer in compromise until after the three years have passed from the assessment date, so that you have the option of filing for bankruptcy (being able to include the taxes) in the event of an offer rejection. Even though you may really be floundering financially, it is bad enough to file for bankruptcy without being allowed to include your tax liability as well.

Case Study:

Wendy is a receptionist and her husband, Craig, a self-employed electrician. The couple had not filed income tax returns for five years. In June of 1990, Craig and Wendy decided to file their past returns and were promptly assessed a tax liability of $50,000. Craig and Wendy did not own their own home and they had virtually no assets. Other than a tax lien, their credit was excellent.

During initial consultation, I informed the couple that if they were considering bankruptcy, they should wait three years from the assessment date, or June of 1993. At that time, Craig and Wendy indicated that they had a very strong objection to filing for bankruptcy so instead entered into an installment agreement in December of 1990, paying the IRS $500 per month.

However, as time progressed the couple realized it would take a very long time to pay off their tax liability and they began to consider bankruptcy. We decided bankruptcy would be a last resort, and started first with an offer in compromise.

Wendy informed me that she had the ability to borrow $10,000 from an uncle. In this circumstance, we deemed the amount to be a reasonable basis for an offer in compromise, even though their liability was still around $50,000. If we had filed the offer prior to June of 1993, we would have extended the statute by approximately one year, adding an additional year of payments of around $6,000. Since we decided the offer had a fair chance of acceptance, we decided to wait until June of 1993 to make the offer so that if it failed Craig and Wendy could immediately file for Chapter 7 bankruptcy, thereby discharging the tax liability.

The other possibility in this case was to immediately make an offer in compromise prior to the installment agreement taking effect. The only problem with this is that generally the IRS prefers to see a good payment history before they will consider an offer in compromise, so Craig and Wendy would have had to make payments for a while to establish integrity (normally six months to a year.)

Usually, the IRS is particularly fond of offers where the monies are coming from third party sources because it's money that they might not normally receive (Craig and Wendy certainly didn't have it). Fortunately, the IRS decided to accept Craig and Wendy's offer, therefore, bankruptcy was not necessary in this case.

Meeting with the Offer Specialist

If you decide to make an offer in compromise you should be aware that you are welcoming an investigation into your financial activities (because offers in compromise are handled by an offer specialist through the collection division). The offer specialist is going to want to meet with you. Offer specialists are very skilled at asking leading questions in order to draw out information - to see if you are hiding anything or in any way trying to dupe the IRS. They are very skilled at questioning integrity and making the innocent feel guilty.

The offer specialist is going to go through a very detailed study of the Form 433A/B that you submitted with your offer and you should be ready with answers.

For instance, regarding the balance sheet information, they will ask you questions about your assets. They will ask about certain items omitted from the asset section - items that most people possess but may not be listed on your balance sheet. For example, let's assume you have a car to drive, but your father owns it and you "rent" it from him. It is not illegal for your father to own the car that you drive. You simply need to know what your answers will be when you meet with the agent.

In terms of liabilities, if you have listed certain debts that you are not currently paying (can't afford to, for example), be prepared to say that you are "trying" to make the payments.

Regarding income, do not include bonuses or commissions that you are not absolutely guaranteed of receiving - no "hopefuls". If you are currently working overtime, let them know that this could end anytime - that there is no guarantee that it will continue. In fact, you suspect overtime hours to end anytime. Do not volunteer information such as, you are working sixty hours per week or can work as many hours as you want. You should stick to a strict forty hour per week income, IF this is what you are working (less, of course, if part-time).

You will need to work very hard for the expense side of your income and expense analysis. Besides the obvious (rent or house payment, utilities, medical insurance, car payment) you will need to include miscellaneous expenses. For example, monies set aside for emergencies, home repairs, car repairs, doctor and dentist bills, veterinary bills if need be. Agents get very "nit-picky" in these areas, but they are legitimate expenses. Stick to your guns and insist on their inclusion.

How to Evaluate the Offer Amount

There are three basic factors that the IRS uses to assess the validity of an offer in compromise. The first two concern the actual calculation of the offer and the third is criteria.

#1. As I've previously stated, page four of form 433A is very important. This is because the IRS will compute the difference between income and expense on the analysis form, multiply the amount of positive cash flow by 60 payments, and expect this amount. (The IRS assumes a five year payment plan, or sixty months.) If your offer is below this amount, chances are it will be rejected.

#2. Another method of determining a valid offer amount is to take the income less expenses (the positive cash flow) from the 433A and multiply that number by the present value of the sixty months, times the current interest rate. (The applicable federal rate is the current interest rate.)

#3. The third factor in determining the validity of an offer amount is your age and current 1040 wages. This is actually a very critical factor; the younger the taxpayer, the higher the offer amount must be because you are more "collectable". (You will live, and therefore work, longer having more time to pay off your tax debt.) If the income and expense difference is a negative cash flow (expenses exceeding income) the IRS will very seriously consider your offer in compromise.

Other Considerations

There is no magic formula to a successful offer in compromise, but there are some other important considerations.

First, the IRS expects any offer to leave you with net assets of *zero*. The balance sheet information on the 433A/B needs to demonstrate that the net assets after the offer will be zero. Remember, if offer monies are being borrowed from a third party source this loan should be listed as a liability on the 433 along with a proposed re-payment plan - even if these monies are later "gifted". In no way do you want to give the IRS the impression that there is an endless supply of monetary resources available to you.

Also, don't make the initial offer your "high" offer. Most times these cases are resolved by negotiating upwards. For example, if you are able to raise $15,000 for an offer, start with a lower offering of $10,000 or $12,000 first. Leave yourself some room for negotiating upwards.

Appeals and Resubmission

If the offer in compromise is rejected by the IRS you have two choices:

#1 Appeal the case to the IRS Appeals Office (see illustration).
#2 Submit a revised offer.

Your appeal should be submitted in duplicate within the 30 day period granted in the IRS rejection letter and should contain the following:
1. A statement that you want to appeal the findings of the rejection letter;
2. Your name and address;
3. The date and symbols referred to in the rejection letter;
4. The tax period(s) or year(s) involved; and
5. A statement of facts supporting your position in any contested factual issue.

This statement of facts must be declared true under penalties of perjury. This may be accomplished by adding to the protest the following signed declaration:

> "Under penalties of perjury, I declare that I have examined the statement of facts presented in this appeal and in any accompanying schedules and statements, and to the best of my knowledge and belief, they are true, correct, and complete."

August 31, 1993

Department of Treasury
Internal Revenue Service
Special Procedures Branch

Attn:

Dear
   We are hereby requesting an appeal on the findings regarding Ima Taxpayer's Offer in Compromise.

   For liabilities assessed to:

   Ima Taxpayer
   SS# 123-45-6789
   Full Address
   Anytown, USA 12345

   The date is August 10, 1993

   The symbols are

   (Both the date and symbols for reference are found on the IRS rejection letter)
   The tax periods the Offer in Compromise covered were 12/31/88 (1040) and 3/31/84 (CIV PEN).

   We are contesting the rejection of the Offer in Compromise because the rejection was based on the taxpayer being able to pay the liability. We feel there was little to no consideration given to the value of the Collateral Agreement.

This agreement has substantial future value combined with the $5000 current Offer is a sound compromise. Considering the prospect of full collection on the assessed liability within the remaining statute, we feel Ima Taxpaper's Offer in Compromise should be taken into consideration.

Jenkins & Company prepared this protest and accompanying documents.

Under penalties of perjury, I declare that I have examined the statement of facts presented in this appeal and in any accompanying schedules and statements, and, to the best of my knowledge and belief, they are true, correct, and complete.

Sincerely,

cc:

Offer In Compromise • 143

If a representative submits the appeal on your behalf (attorney, CPA), he or she may substitute a declaration stating:
1. That he or she prepared the protest and accompanying documents; and
2. Whether he or she knows personally that the statements of fact contained in the accompanying documents are true and correct.

You may represent yourself at the hearing or you may be represented by an attorney, certified public accountant, or an individual enrolled to practice before the Internal Revenue Service. If your representative attends a hearing without you, he or she must file a power of attorney before receiving or inspecting confidential information. Form 2848, Power of Attorney, or other properly written power of attorney may be used for this purpose. Copies of the form can be obtained from any IRS office.

If you decide to submit a revised offer in compromise, the increase should be at least 10% more than the original amount proposed.

If you are handling your tax matters without a tax professional, an important consideration in deciding how to proceed in the event of offer rejection is your relationship with the agent who handled your original offer. If you have developed a good rapport with the agent, then re-submitting an offer would be the proper course of action. On the other hand, if you've found it difficult to work with this agent, an appeal would be more appropriate.

Also, if you appeal your case, it usually takes three to six months for the IRS to respond. *Remember, the offer in compromise* suspends all collection activity, so this will give you extra time to come up with more money. If you decide to resubmit an offer in compromise, collection activity will resume in the interim.

Offer In Compromise • 145

Form **2848**
(Rev. February 1993)
Department of the Treasury
Internal Revenue Service

Power of Attorney and Declaration of Representative
► For Paperwork Reduction and Privacy Act Notice, see the Instructions.

OMB No. 1545-0150
Expires 2-29-96

Part I Power of Attorney (Please type or print.)

1 Taxpayer Information (Taxpayer(s) must sign and date this form on page 2, line 9.)

Taxpayer name(s) and address	Social security number(s)	Employer identification number
	Daytime telephone number ( )	Plan number (if applicable)

hereby appoint(s) the following representative(s) as attorney(s)-in-fact:

2 Representative(s) (Representative(s) must sign and date this form on page 2, Part II.)

Name and address	CAF No. .... Telephone No. ( ) .... Fax No. ( ) .... Check if new: Address ☐ Telephone No. ☐
Name and address	CAF No. .... Telephone No. ( ) .... Fax No. ( ) .... Check if new: Address ☐ Telephone No. ☐
Name and address	CAF No. .... Telephone No. ( ) .... Fax No. ( ) .... Check if new: Address ☐ Telephone No. ☐

to represent the taxpayer(s) before the Internal Revenue Service for the following tax matters:

3 Tax Matters

Type of Tax (Income, Employment, Excise, etc.)	Tax Form Number (1040, 941, 720, etc.)	Year(s) or Period(s)

4 Specific Use Not Recorded on Centralized Authorization File (CAF).— If the power of attorney is for a specific use not recorded on CAF, please check this box. (See **Line 4—Specific Uses Not Recorded on CAF** on page 3.). . . . . ► ☐

5 Acts Authorized.—The representatives are authorized to receive and inspect confidential tax information and to perform any and all acts that I (we) can perform with respect to the tax matters described in line 3, for example, the authority to sign any agreements, consents, or other documents. The authority does not include the power to receive refund checks (see line 6 below) or the power to sign certain returns (see **Line 5—Acts Authorized** on page 4).
List any specific additions or deletions to the acts otherwise authorized in this power of attorney: ....
....
....

Note: *In general, an unenrolled preparer of tax returns cannot sign any document for a taxpayer. See Revenue Procedure 81-38, printed as Pub. 470, for more information.*
Note: *The tax matters partner/person of a partnership or S corporation is not permitted to authorize representatives to perform certain acts. See the instructions for more information.*

6 Receipt of Refund Checks.—If you want to authorize a representative named in line 2 to receive, **BUT NOT TO ENDORSE OR CASH**, refund checks, initial here _____ and list the name of that representative below.

Name of representative to receive refund check(s) ►

Cat. No. 11980J

Form **2848** (Rev. 2-93)

4-5-93 Published by Tax Management Inc., a Subsidiary of The Bureau of National Affairs, Inc. 2848.1

146 • FAILURE TO FILE

Form 2848 (Rev. 2-93)   Page 2

7 Notices and Communications.—Notices and other written communications will be sent to the first representative listed in line 2.
  a If you also want the second representative listed to receive such notices and communications, check this box . . . ▶ ☐
  b If you do not want any notices or communications sent to your representative, check this box . . . . ▶ ☐

8 Retention/Revocation of Prior Power(s) of Attorney.—The filing of this power of attorney automatically revokes all earlier power(s) of attorney on file with the Internal Revenue Service for the same tax matters and years or periods covered by this document. If you do not want to revoke a prior power of attorney, check here . . . . ▶ ☐
  YOU MUST ATTACH A COPY OF ANY POWER OF ATTORNEY YOU WANT TO REMAIN IN EFFECT.

9 Signature of Taxpayer(s).—If a tax matter concerns a joint return, **both** husband and wife must sign if joint representation is requested, otherwise, see the instructions. If signed by a corporate officer, partner, guardian, tax matters partner/person, executor, receiver, administrator, or trustee on behalf of the taxpayer, I certify that I have the authority to execute this form on behalf of the taxpayer.

▶ **IF THIS POWER OF ATTORNEY IS NOT SIGNED AND DATED, IT WILL BE RETURNED.**

_____   _____   _____
          Signature   Date   Title (if applicable)

_____
          Print Name

_____   _____   _____
          Signature   Date   Title (if applicable)

_____
          Print Name

Part II Declaration of Representative

Under penalties of perjury, I declare that:
- I am not currently under suspension or disbarment from practice before the Internal Revenue Service;
- I am aware of regulations contained in Treasury Department Circular No. 230 (31 CFR, Part 10), as amended, concerning the practice of attorneys, certified public accountants, enrolled agents, enrolled actuaries, and others;
- I am authorized to represent the taxpayer(s) identified in Part I for the tax matter(s) specified there; and
- I am one of the following:
  a **Attorney**—a member in good standing of the bar of the highest court of the jurisdiction shown below.
  b **Certified Public Accountant**—duly qualified to practice as a certified public accountant in the jurisdiction shown below.
  c **Enrolled Agent**—enrolled as an agent under the requirements of Treasury Department Circular No. 230.
  d **Officer**—a bona fide officer of the taxpayer organization.
  e **Full-Time Employee**—a full-time employee of the taxpayer.
  f **Family Member**—a member of the taxpayer's immediate family (i.e., spouse, parent, child, brother, or sister).
  g **Enrolled Actuary**—enrolled as an actuary by the Joint Board for the Enrollment of Actuaries under 29 U.S.C. 1242 (the authority to practice before the Service is limited by section 10.3(d)(1) of Treasury Department Circular No. 230).
  h **Unenrolled Return Preparer**—an unenrolled return preparer under section 10.7(a)(7) of Treasury Department Circular No. 230.

▶ If this declaration of representative is not signed and dated, the power of attorney will be returned.

Designation —Insert above letter (a–h)	Jurisdiction (state) or Enrollment Card No.	Signature	Date

2848.2   Published by Tax Management Inc., a Subsidiary of The Bureau of National Affairs, Inc.   4-5-93

June 15, 1993

Internal Revenue Service
Cincinnati, OH 45999

RE: Jack D. & Jill B Taxpayer
383-28-4553

Gentlemen:

I have been retained by Mr. and Mrs. Taxpayer to prepare their tax returns for the years 1988 thru 1992.

I will submit the returns as soon as they are completed.

Enclosed please find a power of attorney. If you have any questions regarding this matter, please contact my office.

Sincerely,

JAMES E. JENKINS, C.P.A.

JEJ/jk
Encl.
CC: Mr and Mrs. Taxpayer

*He saw a Lawyer killing a viper
On a dunghill hard by his own stable;
And the Devil smiled, for it put him in mind
Of Cain and his brother, Abel.*
-    *Samuel Taylor Coleridge*

8

Bankruptcy

THE MAIN GOAL of this chapter is to make you aware of when bankruptcy may be an appropriate course of action. Also, how to choose a competent bankruptcy attorney.

Bankruptcy is usually a course of last resort when such things as payment arrangements and offers in compromise fail. Even though bankruptcy is not the first mode d'employ to consider, it is a viable option to keep in mind. Paradoxically, in many instances it may save a person's financial life.

Initially, many of my clients have the hope of setting up some type of payment arrangement with the IRS, only to become despondent after seeing the huge amounts of interest and penalties than can accrue. Imagine having a visa card balance of forty or fifty thousand dollars and trying to make a dent in the principle. Nobody wants to be a bad guy and file bankruptcy. Certainly, it is a kiss of death on a credit report, but a tax lien or two can do equal damage. After considering all avenues - and struggling to keep a payment arrangement for three years - many people do opt for bankruptcy.

It is not my goal to be a bankruptcy attorney nor was this book designed to be the expert reference in terms of bankruptcy. Therefore, nothing I say should be considered legal advice. However, I feel it is necessary to cover certain options regarding bankruptcy and provide some sort of guidance in this area.

Chapter Seven Bankruptcy

First of all, it is important to note that each State has exemptions regarding bankruptcy that allows the person filing to retain certain assets. To find out what these local laws are, contact a bankruptcy attorney.

Generally speaking, and put rather simply, Chapter 7 bankruptcy is a complete liquidation of all assets and liability. Generally speaking, income taxes are a priority item in a Chapter 7 bankruptcy (not dischargeable). However, as mentioned previously, income taxes lose their priority status three years from the assessment date of the tax. Also, if you file Chapter 7 bankruptcy *before* the three year period (when taxes are still a priority item) the bankruptcy *does* dismiss interest and penalties, leaving only the base tax liability. This can be a great relief considering that interest and penalties can account for 50% of the tax debt.

I have found that in many nonfiler cases taxpayers owe the Government more money than they can ever possibly hope to pay. This problem is compounded by the various waves of IRS penalties and interest. For all practical purposes, many nonfilers may as well owe the entire national deficit because in many instances they simply are not going to be able to pay their tax debt.

The ability to discharge tax debt under the bankruptcy statute is a very important rule. Let's return to one of the first case studies in this book, John our computer salesman (Chapter One). John is probably a perfect candidate for Chapter 7 bankruptcy. In his case, as in so many, it may be *possible* for him to pay off his tax debt over a ten year period, but his life would be absolutely miserable. If John decided to file for bankruptcy and he had a tax assessment date of April 15, 1993, he wouldn't be able to file for bankruptcy until April 15, 1996, when his income taxes could be dischargeable under the bankruptcy statute.

Important

Remember, in order to incorporate a tax liability into a bankruptcy, the returns must first be filed so that there is a tax assessment date. IRS assessed taxes do not count; a 90 day letter with IRS assessed tax is not a filed return. For example, in the case of Bill (our tax protestor from Chapter One), even though the IRS has assessed him more than $400,000 in taxes (an amount he will never be able to pay) it would be impossible for him to file Chapter 7 and relieve himself of the tax burden simply because he has never filed his tax returns.

So, if you have IRS assessed tax liabilities (perhaps from 1984-1985), especially with huge interest and penalties, you will need to file your tax returns in order to get the statute period started. Wait three years before filing a Chapter 7 so that the taxes can be discharged, and deal with the IRS as best as possible in the interim.

The Automatic Stay

In terms of tax debt, one benefit of filing for bankruptcy is the *automatic stay*. The filing of a bankruptcy petition triggers an automatic stay, which precludes creditors from taking actions to enforce the collection of certain liabilities. It is one of the fundamental debtor protections provided by the Bankruptcy Code.

Specifically, the automatic stay prohibits the IRS from:
* Assessing a prepetition tax deficiency against the debtor;
* Setting off a prepetition tax refund against a tax liability owed by the debtor;
* Filing a tax lien, levying, or taking any other collection action against the debtor or against the debtor's property for a prepetition tax liability; or
* Filing a notice of tax lien or taking any other collection action against the property of the bankruptcy estate.

However, there are also limitations to the automatic stay. It does not preclude the IRS from:
* Issuing a notice of deficiency;
* Assessing and collecting postpetition taxes that are not subject to the notice of deficiency procedures; or
* Refiling a notice of tax lien.

Chapter Thirteen

Chapter 13 bankruptcy is a reorganization of debt, with equal payments being spread out over a period of five years (sixty months). It is limited to individual taxpayers with regular income, but married taxpayers can file a joint Chapter 13 petition. Relief under Chapter 13 is also available to taxpayers who operate businesses as sole proprietorships. To qualify for Chapter 13 relief, your debts must not exceed $100,000 for unsecured debts and $350,000 for secured debts. The typical Chapter 13 case is initiated by an individual at the lower end of the income scale and is often filed to stave off foreclosure of the family home. Note: In Chapter 13 bankruptcy, *all postpetition* taxes must be paid currently. This means that you will need to stay current with current taxes once you file the Chapter 13 bankruptcy petition. If you don't stay current with current taxes, the Chapter 13 will be converted to a Chapter 7 for a complete liquidation of all assets and liability.

Case Study:

Mark was a self-employed commissioned salesman and Jackie was a homemaker. By nature of his business, Mark would receive large commission checks and then experience long period with no cash flow. Mark filed his income tax returns (after not filing for a three year period) resulting in an $80,000 tax liability.

Mark and Jackie made payment arrangements with the IRS. In order to secure their position, the IRS filed a lien against the couple's personal residence. Mark and Jackie failed at the payment arrangement several times because of Mark's sporadic cash flow, and the IRS informed Mark that they intended to auction off the couple's home.

Filing a Chapter 7 bankruptcy wouldn't work in this case, because the IRS had already placed a lien on their home, meaning the IRS was actually in a position where they would be collecting the monies. Also, Mark and the IRS were not able to agree on an acceptable payment that the couple could actually live with. This was a perfect time to file for Chapter 13, which would force the IRS to accept equal installments over a five year period of time and enable the couple to keep their home.

There was also another important timing consideration in this case: I originally met with Mark and Jackie in November of 1992. At this time, they hadn't paid any of their current (1992) taxes either, so an additional $15,000 was due on April 15, 1993. Remember, once in a Chapter 13 all postpetition taxes must be paid currently. Since Mark and Jackie could in no way pay the 1992 taxes, it was important to wait until the end of the current tax year (12-31-92) so that they could be included in the Chapter 13 petition along with the other past due taxes.

On a purely tactical basis (temporarily appeasing the IRS) I called the agent assigned to their case, setting up a payment arrangement. This was done in December. I made the payments ridiculously high, with the first payment due January 20, 1993, and the agent accepted. We knew Mark and Jackie couldn't possibly keep the arrangement, but it got us into January 1993 where we could file Chapter 13, taking the matter completely out of the hands of the IRS and into the jurisdiction of the bankruptcy courts.

Case Study:
Judy is a doctor who had filed for Chapter 7 bankruptcy some years earlier, but still owed a substantial amount of

payroll and recent income taxes totalling around $60,000. It was not beyond her means to pay off the debt, but she needed fairly generous terms. In the past, she had entered into four or five payment arrangements with the IRS but had failed at each one. The IRS was particularly upset when she failed to make her current estimated 1992 income tax payments of an additional $12,000. The Government decided they would no longer work with Judy, but wanted to liquidate her completely. This meant going after any and all assets, including Blue Cross and medicare/medicaid payments from the insurance companies. The IRS planned to auction off her practice and completely put her out of business.

The only thing to do, given Judy's circumstances, was to file Chapter 13 bankruptcy. Certainly, this was a last resort tactic, but doing so allowed Judy to keep her practice and pay the Government equal installments over a five year period of time.

Chapter "Twenty"

There is, of course, no such thing as a Chapter 20 bankruptcy, but this is the standard term used for a combination of Chapter 7 and Chapter 13 bankruptcies.

The Chapter 20 is probably best explained by using an example:

Let's assume you have a total debt of around $200,000 and literally no assets. You're getting a tremendous amount of pressure from creditors, one of which is the IRS (to whom you owe $50,000 of that total debt). You cannot reorganize this debt under Chapter 13 because the amount is over $100,000. Even though a good portion of the tax debt is not yet 3 years old (therefore not dischargeable under the Bankruptcy Statute) it would be a good idea to go ahead and file Chapter 7, just to give yourself some relief. The Chapter 7 would discharge all non-priority debts, including interest and penalties from the tax debt (but not the base tax). After filing a Chapter 7, it may shrink the tax liability to $30,000 (or the original base tax). Then, the following day, you could file a Chapter 13 reorganizing the remaining debt over a five year period, making your life just a bit more tolerable.

The Bankruptcy Attorney

Since it is not my job to be a bankruptcy attorney, it would be helpful to give you some advice on finding someone competent.

As in any profession, bankruptcy attorneys seem to run anywhere from outstanding to pathetic in terms of competency. It is extremely important to work with an attorney who is not only familiar with bankruptcy law, but is also very familiar with statutes and tax law as they pertain to bankruptcy. This won't be your standard out-of-the-newspaper attorney.

The attorney's knowledge of tax law is paramount. I know of cases where an unlearned lawyer played the bankruptcy "card" with disastrous results concerning an individual's tax liability. If the lawyer had simply waited one more year on the tax assessment date, the taxes could have been discharged along with the other debt. If a lawyer files for bankruptcy too soon, it could mean keeping the IRS claim alive for the full ten year statutory period. It's bad enough for an individual to have to file for bankruptcy in the first place, only to find that they may still owe the Government for back taxes.

I have also seen cases where income taxes should have been dischargeable in bankruptcy, but the attorney failed to include the IRS debt on the petition and an individual continued in their payment arrangement with the IRS. Or, the taxes were dischargeable and included in the bankruptcy petition, but the IRS was not informed (and therefore not present at the hearing) so the collection agents continued taking action against the individual. In cases such as these, the attorney needed to make a *separate* motion before the judge in order to clear the tax liability.

For these reasons it is imperative to research and find a bankruptcy attorney that you feel is competent. A good way to do this is to call your local bar association and/or interview a potential bankruptcy attorney. Some questions to ask are:

1. Can you supply me with references of satisfied clients?
2. How many bankruptcies do you file in a year?
3. How many of those bankruptcies concern tax liability?
4. Are you familiar with tax law? and the bankruptcy statute as pertaining to the discharge of taxes?

Also, you could pose some "what if" scenarios from your own situation. After having read this book, you should know enough about statutes and strategies to ascertain whether your attorney is knowledgeable of the same or simply a "run of the mill" lawyer who simply files a bankruptcy petition without regard to now and future strategy.

"I've never seen a nonfiler situation that couldn't be solved."
 - *James Jenkins, CPA*

9

Help When You Need It

IT'S ONE THING to read a book, but quite another to apply the strategies, advice, and information to your specific circumstance. Many times things sound clear at first-reading, but when you try to incorporate that information into a real-life scenario, issues can quickly become clouded.

That's one reason I started *Tax Research Services, Inc.,* an extensive library of information that is updated continually. We also offer specific advice to difficult questions. Tax Research Services (TRS) has a network of 25 plus experts including a bankruptcy attorney, a tax attorney, an actuary and insurance professionals.

When you purchased this book, you also received a one-time opportunity to use TRS *free of charge* for any nonfiling question. When you call our number (1-800-333-TAXX) you will speak directly to a CPA. Usually your question can be answered immediately (the average phone call is four minutes). If more research is required we can call you back, usually the same day. Also, at your request, we will supply the supporting documentation by either mailing or faxing the hard copy of the researched material.

160 • Failure To File

Your first call with a nonfiling question will be free. After that, the standard fee is only $5.00 per minute, and since each call averages four minutes, that's only $20.00 to get an answer to a difficult tax question. You are *not* charged for the research time.

This service is normally used only by tax professionals, but it is now being made available to nonfiling consumers. Here's what some of our clients have said about Tax Research Services:

"...TRS proved to be a quick, convenient and handy source when time was a priority."
Dana Stahl, CPA, Port Clinton, Ohio

"...I cut my reference services by 75%, reducing overhead! We use TRS several times monthly - even after tax season. By the time it takes to walk to my library and pick out a reference book, I could have dialed Tax Research Services."
Rosalie A. Mudgett
Windsor Tax Service, Eidersburg, Maryland

"...TRS is invaluable, especially when dealing with rush projects... Questions have been answered expediently and completely with code sections when needed... I recommend the service to others."
T. Kirk Blaner, The Accountants Desk
Phoenix, Arizona

"...TRS provided valuable cites and insights, and has acted as a sounding board when I've needed an impartial or second opinion or fresh perspective..."
Joseph M. Beninghof, CFP, MST
JMB Financial & Tax Strategies, Avon, Connecticut

Another service provided by TRS (at a minimal fee) is a complete supply of federal, state, and local tax forms - especially useful when you haven't filed your tax returns for a number of years. The IRS doesn't even have many of the forms needed for the filing of past income tax returns. TRS carries forms going back to the 1970's and state forms for all fifty states.

Remember, help is available if you need it, and your first call is free.

Tax Research Services, Inc.
1-800-333-TAXX
Visa, Mastercard, American Express, Discover

Glossary

Automated Collection Service (ACS)
A computer-based on-line inventory of delinquent tax accounts and delinquent tax investigations for tax liabilities under $10,000. ACS call sites are responsible for the resolution and collection of delinquent accounts and for securing delinquent returns through concentrated telephone contacts.

Automatic Stay, The
One of the fundamental debtor protections provided by the Bankruptcy Code. The filing of a bankruptcy petition triggers an automatic stay, which precludes creditors from taking actions to enforce the collection of certain liabilities.

Bankruptcy Statute of Limitations
This statute allows the discharge of taxes in bankruptcy after the tax assessment is at least three years old. Under Chapter 7, if bankruptcy is filed before the tax assessment is three years old, the interest and penalties would, however, be dischargeable.

Chapter Seven Bankruptcy
Rather simply, a complete liquidation of all assets and liability. (Generally speaking, income taxes are a priority item but after three years from their assessment date lose their priority and are dischargeable.)

Chapter Thirteen Bankruptcy

A reorganization of debt with equal payments being spread out over a period of five years (sixty months). It is limited to individual taxpayers with regular income, but married taxpayers can file a joint Chapter 13 petition. Also available to taxpayers who operate businesses as sole proprietorships. To qualify, debts must not exceed $100,000 for unsecured debts and $350,000 for secured debts.

Chapter "Twenty" Bankruptcy

A term used for a combination of Chapter 7 and Chapter 13 bankruptcies, used strategically in the best interest of a client.

Collectable Liability

A right to collect a tax liability (by levy, lien, or garnishee of bank accounts) established by the IRS by issuing a 90 day letter in which a taxpayer is informed of his or her tax liability along with a direct demand of payment.

Collection Information Statement (Forms 433A and 433B)

Forms used to outline a taxpayer's (433A) or business' (433B) income and expenses in order to come up with a payment arrangement with the IRS Collection Division.

Friendly Lien, The

The placing of a lien against a property by a "friendly" party (family, friends) as security for a genuine loan in order to protect assets from lien by the Internal Revenue Service, rendering the IRS lien ineffective and usually greatly diminishing the threat of eventual seizure.

Levy

An administrative collection technique that is an actual seizure of funds. Usually done electronically, the IRS can remove all cash from an individual's bank account, or deduct money from an individual's wages.

Lien

The most widely used method of IRS administrative collection techniques. The lien is not an actual seizure of property but rather places a security interest in a taxpayer's property for taxes owed. (See Friendly Lien.)

Ninety Day Letter

IRS prepared returns assessing a taxpayer's tax liability and giving the taxpayer 90 days to dispute the taxes. Otherwise, the IRS assessment will become final with no recourse (very few exceptions are ever made).

Nonfiler Program

A program initiated by the IRS in October 1992 designed to locate nonfilers and recoup delinquent taxes.

Nonfiling Syndrome

Minor to extreme feelings of guilt, paranoia, depression and anxiety directly due to the nonfiling of income tax returns and fear of possible consequences by the Internal Revenue Service.

Offer in Compromise

An attempt to settle a tax debt for a lesser amount than the actual liability. All collection activity is suspended during this time, but so is the statute of limitations, plus an additional six months is added.

Offer Period, The

That time between the filing of the offer in compromise until the time that the offer is either accepted or rejected. Usually 4 to 6 months.

Overall Strategy

A total review of a client's tax status, financial status, and extent of IRS action that greatly determines tactical decisions. Best summed up as "not necessarily the lowest tax on the 1040, but the lowest OVERALL financial liability with priority given to the protection of assets".

Point of No Return
The point at which it is mathematically impossible or near impossible for a taxpayer to repay his or her tax liability, based on such factors as the amount of tax owed, the taxpayer's income, the number of years the taxpayer has yet to work before retirement or death, while trying to maintain an acceptable standard of living.

Postfiling Strategies
Strategies designed to protect a client's assets and financial well-being during the collection process (after the filing of the tax returns).

Power of Attorney (Form 2848)
Written legal authority to act for another person.

Prefiling Strategies
Strategies attempting to financially position a client as favorably as possible prior to the filing of the income tax returns.

Saddam Hussein Syndrome
Author-coined idiom referring to the mind-set of a tax protestor who decides to challenge the U.S. Government.

Statute of Limitations
See Bankruptcy Statute of Limitations
See Ten Year Statute of Limitations

Summons Power
The ability of the IRS to summon information, either the actual completed tax returns or income information in order to prepare the returns. Generally, a court order is not needed to obtain this information.

Tax Court Petition
The solution and only response to a 90 day letter which disputes the taxes as assessed by the IRS.

Tax Research Services, Inc.
A library reference service founded by the author that also provides tax opinions and advice, and out-dated tax forms for the filing of back returns.

Ten Day Letter
A letter issued by the IRS informing a taxpayer that if he or she does not respond to the IRS within ten days the IRS will estimate their tax liability.

Ten Year Statute of Limitations
According to the Revenue Reconciliation Act of 1990, the IRS has ten years to collect taxes after their assessment - whether through administrative collection (levy, seizure) or initiate a judicial collection proceeding (institute a suit for collection of a taxpayer's unpaid federal tax liability).

Thirty Day Letter
A letter issued by the IRS notifying a taxpayer of a proposed tax liability (based on IRS records). The taxpayer has thirty days to dispute this tax calculation as estimated by the IRS. A ninety day letter will follow.

We the People ACT (American Citizens Tribunal)
An anti-tax group formed in the early eighties comprised of approximately 7,500 auto workers in the Pontiac and Flint areas. This group caused one of the largest tax revolts in U.S. History.

Index

Appeals, 140,143
Attorney, 156,157
Automated Collection Service
   (ACS), 121,122
Automatic Stay, 152

Bankruptcy
   Attorney, 156,157
   Chapter Seven, 150,151
   Chapter Thirteen, 152-155
   Chapter "Twenty", 155,156
   Statute (See Statute of
   Limitations)
Bob and Weave, 124
Buying Time, 46,47,50,123

Chapter Seven (See Bankruptcy)
Chapter Thirteen
   (See Bankruptcy)
Chapter "Twenty"
   (See Bankruptcy)
Collectable, 139
Collectable Liability, 32
Collection, 105
   Agents, 119-121
   Suspension of, 134,142,143
Collection Information
   Statement, 106-116
      Computing Expense, 106-108
      Computing Income, 106-108
Criminal Intent, 37

Dischargeable (See Tax)

Failed Payment Arrangements,
   96,97,124-127,152-155
Financial Difficulties, 7-9
Financially Dysfunctional, 80,81
Friendly Lien, 100,101

Gathering Information, 50,51

Income and Expense Analysis,
   106-108,117-119
Ineffective Lien, 100,101
Initial Contact, 22-27
Installment Agreement Request,
   117,118
   (See Payment Arrangements)

Levy, 81,82,124-127
   Exemptions, 84,85
   Bank & Security Accounts,
      81,82,93
   Ineffective, 100,101
   Release, 83
   Wages, 82
Lien, 85,86
   Friendly, 100,101
   Release, 87
   Security Interest, 85

Married Filing Jointly, 95-97

Married Filing Separately, 97,98
Missing Information, 66

Ninety Day Letter, 28,31,32,71,72
Nonfiler Program, 20,21
Nonfilers, 4,7-16,19,20
    Locating, 21,22
Nonfiling Syndrome, 5,6

Offer In Compromise,
    129-133,136-139
    Advantage, 131,134
    Amount, 138,139
    Appeal, 140-143
    Disadvantage, 134
    Period, 131
    Rejection, 140
    Resubmission, 140-143
    Timing, 134,135,143,144
Overall Strategy, 39-45

Payment Arrangement, 78,96,97,
    107,108,117,119,124
    Default/Failed, 124-127
    (See Installment Agreement)
Penalties, 76,77
    Punitive, 76,77
    Waiver, 79-81
Postpetition Taxes, 153
Power Of Attorney, 143-147
Prefiling Strategies, 89-101
    Married Both Employed,
    100,101
    Married Filing Jointly, 95-97
    Married Filing Separately,
    97,98
    Married Self Employed, 99
    Married Unemployed, 94
    Reorganization Of Ownership, 98,99
    Single Employed Mobile,
    92,93

Single Self Employed 94,95
Single Stationary Employment, 90-92
Single Unemployed, 94
Priority Item (See Taxes)
Procrastinators, 10-12

Reality Check, 78
Resubmission (See Offer In
    Compromise)
Reorganization Of Ownership,
    98,99
Reward, 22

Saddam Hussein Syndrome, 13
Security Interest (See Lien)
Seizure (See Levy)
Strategies (See Prefiling)
Statute of Limitations
    Bankruptcy, 46
    Ten Year, 45
Summons Power, 33-37

Tax Court Petition, 71-76
Tax Organizer, 50,52-65
Tax Professional (hiring of),
    40,41
Tax Protestors, 12-16
Tax Research Service, Inc.,
    101,159-161
Tax Returns
    Aggressive Approach, 67,68
    Conservative Approach, 67,68
Taxes
    Assessment of, 45
    Discharge of, 46
    Forms, 101,161
    Postpetition, 153
    Priority Item (Status) 46
    Refunds, 16
Ten Day Letter, 22,28,29
Thirty Day Letter, 28,30